Do Not Cast Me Away

Do Not Cast Me Away

Dementia in the Congregation

Paul Rader

WIPF & STOCK · Eugene, Oregon

DO NOT CAST ME AWAY
Dementia in the Congregation

Copyright © 2020 Paul Rader. All rights reserved. Except for brief quotations in critical publications or reviews, no part of this book may be reproduced in any manner without prior written permission from the publisher. Write: Permissions, Wipf and Stock Publishers, 199 W. 8th Ave., Suite 3, Eugene, OR 97401.

Wipf & Stock
An Imprint of Wipf and Stock Publishers
199 W. 8th Ave., Suite 3
Eugene, OR 97401

www.wipfandstock.com

PAPERBACK ISBN: 978-1-7252-5176-2
HARDCOVER ISBN: 978-1-7252-5177-9
EBOOK ISBN: 978-1-7252-5178-6

Manufactured in the U.S.A.   05/07/20

To Linda,
Lindsey, Gresha, and Thomas,
the loves of my life.

Do not cast me away when I am old;
do not forsake me when my strength is gone.

—PSALM 71:9

Contents

Introduction ... ix

1. Susan and Charlie ... 1
2. Causes of Dementia ... 8
3. The Big Three Causes ... 16
4. Memory ... 25
5. Assessment ... 33
6. Kinds of Care ... 41
7. Memory Care ... 49
8. Guilt ... 57
9. Paying for Care ... 65
10. Finding Support ... 74
11. Elder Abuse ... 83
12. Saying Goodbye ... 93

Penultimate Thoughts ... 101
Suggested Resources ... 109
Bibliography ... 111

Introduction

AFTER A HECTIC MORNING at home watering the yard, jogging with the dog, returning phone calls, and checking email, I hopped in my car and drove toward church and suddenly realized that I could not remember if I had turned off the water sprinkler. I tried to call a neighbor to check for me, but she did not answer her phone. There was nothing else to do. Reluctantly I turned around. As I had feared, a steady spray of water was moving back and forth across a patch of newly planted grass. "I must be getting Alzheimer's," I told myself, as I got out of the car to do what I thought I had already done.

Isn't that one of the things we say when we forget something? Once upon a time we would say we were distracted, or multitasking, or had ADD, or just weren't paying attention. But with age comes the terrifying specter of dementia.

According to information on the Alzheimer's Association's website, the quick facts are these: Alzheimer's disease is the sixth leading cause of death in the United States; one in three seniors dies with Alzheimer's or some other dementia; and Alzheimer's disease is the only cause of death in the top ten in America that cannot be prevented, slowed, or cured. In 2015 Alzheimer's and other dementias cost our nation $226 billion. By 2050, these costs could rise as high as $1.1 trillion.

Dementias not only affect individuals and their families; they plague us in other kinds of ways, as well. What happens when the owner of the most important company in town begins

Introduction

to be affected? Or a surgeon at the hospital? Or the pastor of your church? No place that involves people is immune. If dementia has not come to your pulpit, it will. It most assuredly has arrived already in your congregation.

Fresh out of seminary (in 1984) I was called to be the Associate Pastor of First Presbyterian Church in Ashland, Kentucky. Part of that proud congregation's legacy is the longevity of two of its senior pastors: W. C. Condit and Samuel R. Curry. Condit served an amazing fifty-five years, from 1866 to 1921; Curry served for thirty-six years. Being a history buff, I did a fair amount of digging into the careers of these two men, and as Curry retired in 1963, there were dozens of church members who remembered him. (There were a few who remembered Condit, too!)

But, whereas Condit was spoken of with the reverence one would expect of a beloved figure, there was a blight of sorts when it came to Curry. The stated reason for his retirement was poor health. Those who kept up with him afterward remarked that he was hospitalized for an extended period of time near the end of his life. Several people said they made an effort to visit him in the hospital (or later in a nursing home) but finally gave up because it distressed them so. He had a loud voice and "could be heard bellowing" down the hallway, shouting "the most hateful things." Years later I realized he must have suffered from some form of dementia.

Dementia has been present in every congregation I have served—in Ashland, Kentucky; Huntington, West Virginia; Knoxville, Tennessee; and Chattanooga, Tennessee. In one case, I suspect it was in the pulpit. It may be in yours, too. For certain, it is in your congregation. Dealing with dementia may be the greatest health care challenge facing our generation. It is a theological challenge, too: What does it mean to be human if we can no longer think? Does a demented person reflect the image of God? The children of Israel were enjoined to remember their captivity in Egypt and to remember their deliverance, and the church remembers the death and resurrection of Jesus Christ every time it celebrates communion. What is the implication for our faith if we cannot remember?

Introduction

I began working on this book as a way to guide my own efforts in ministry with people with dementia and their caregivers. The time I put in on it would not have been possible without love and support from my wife, Linda, and the generosity of numerous church members and their families who let me into their lives. In the pages that follow I will explore (among other things) what dementia is, how to recognize it, what it does to people, and how families and church communities deal with it. I will share some of the ways it unfolded in people I cared for and in families I love. I admit at the outset that what follows will in no way be comprehensive.

Ultimately, the aim of this book is to demystify dementia in order to encourage people and congregations to respond to it in meaningful, helpful, and faithful ways. This is a conversation we all need to enter. Like it or not, dealing with dementia is now part of the stewardship of our lives together. As people and as congregations, it's what we do: deal with what comes our way, and care for one another no matter what.

1

Susan and Charlie

> "I've been wondering," Isabelle commented reflectively over dessert, "if it is foolish to make new memories when you know you are going to lose them."
>
> —ERICA BAUERMEISTER,
> *THE SCHOOL OF ESSENTIAL INGREDIENTS*

I WAS HALF LISTENING to the evening news while fixing dinner one evening when I heard a name mentioned that I knew. Then another familiar name, then a voice I recognized. Sliding around the counter from the kitchen to the sitting room where our television stood, I saw Charlie and Susan Smith, members of a church I had previously served, being interviewed for participating in a "Walk to End Alzheimer's."

Charlie and Susan

I was thrilled. Charlie and Susan were two of my favorite people. They had moved from Kingsport to Knoxville while I was at First Presbyterian, Knoxville. He was a retired chemical engineer; she had worked for Holston Presbytery. Their son, Preston, his wife, Emily, and their family had been among the younger couples at First Church. When *their* son Charlie (named after his granddad) was little, my wife and I babysat him a few times.

My elation over seeing them interviewed faded as I caught on to the reason they had been singled out. I heard Susan say, "It's a slow progressing, which is nice. He does everything for himself. I can leave him home; there's no problem. He can fix himself a meal, he can clean up after himself, too. He's very good at that."

A few months later I found myself in their living room. Charlie was in the early stages of Alzheimer's disease, and they were remarkably candid about it all. Susan said even before they moved to Knoxville, she had a suspicion that something was amiss. She said Charlie would say or do something that was out of character, but it would be a small thing that she would forget about until the next occurrence.

Eventually she brought it up with their family physician. He told her that Charlie seemed perfectly normal in his brief interactions with him, but that she should keep track of "incidents" that she could tell him about later. He would investigate based on her observations.

The realization that something is wrong with a person, that a loved one isn't thinking correctly, is one of the most difficult issues anyone has to face. It was hard for Susan, as you can imagine. And Charlie began to take his own "creeping" dementia seriously after having a conversation with Preston about an event that didn't happen. He thought it had; Preston assured him it hadn't. This put the whole family on alert.

Charlie Smith is a brilliant man. If any person could turn back the tides of Alzheimer's by sheer brain power, Charlie could. His area of expertise was explosives, and his lab developed something known as RDX and HMX, used by our military in Vietnam and afterwards. He is still able to work a daily crossword puzzle in ink, but he has clearly slowed down. He was always quiet and thoughtful; now he is doubly so.

Susan and Charlie

Susan shared with me a comment he made to her that I suspect most caregivers have heard. She was explaining to him something going on with her brother-in-law who was ill. Charlie did not remember that the brother-in-law had had leukemia for years. She told him that she realized he might forget what she told him and would remind him if he wished. He said that he wanted her to remind him. Then he said, "You know, I forget that I forget."

One of his first decisions after coming to grips with his illness was to give up his car keys. "Sold my car, bought a new refrigerator" was how he put it. The family says it was more involved than that, but he had the right idea.

As I talked with the two of them about their television interview and the reason for it, I couldn't help but marvel at how normal they appeared.

Susan's Letter

A week or so after my visit with them, Susan sent me the following letter. I have her permission to reprint it below.

> Paul,
>
> Charlie and I enjoyed our visit with you last week and appreciate you for coming. We will be interested in reading your book!
>
> When you were here, I did think of the differences in what I would say if Charlie had not been in the room! Our family is adamant about respecting Charlie's feelings and giving him the respect he should have. We are careful what we say in his presence. We are not hesitant to remind him that he does have Alzheimer's and that it does present some challenges. He does not realize that most of the time and it is very difficult for him when he realizes that he is confused.
>
> The preserving of a person's dignity is one of the most important tasks of a caregiver; I take this very seriously as does our family.

Do Not Cast Me Away

From what I read on the caregivers site of which I am a part, many others feel the same. It can be a challenge but it can be done. This is perceived differently by different people, of course; it is interesting to read what people think about it.

Unknown to Charlie, we sometimes have family meetings—just the adults. That would include Preston, Emily, Erin, Kirk, my sister and brother-in-law, and me. Sometimes there is a specific topic or concern and sometimes it is a matter of being in touch about Charlie and figuring out if we are doing what we need to do. It also is a way for me to express how I am doing and if there is anything I need from any or all of them. Usually we are all there—it is harder for Kirk to make it if we meet for lunch but he is OK about us meeting without him. I am grateful that this group is able to be really honest with each other. Sometimes they express specific concerns about me—am I taking care of myself, what do I think about whatever, what do I think about the possibility of ??? The support from our family and friends is priceless. I am part of a group of five women; we have known each other for more than 40 years. These women are major supporters of me and of Charlie and I am most appreciative.

Had Charlie not been present and you had asked about the changes that had taken place for me, I would have added that I am usually more like a mom now. That is more from necessity and from just being responsible for everything rather than how Charlie treats me. He still treats me as if I am special and I treasure that.

At this time, relatively speaking, we do not have huge problems with which to cope. I know that may change—probably will. Charlie does really well taking care of himself; he is accepting and easy going on the whole. He does stand his ground on some things—such as his refusal to use his walker when we go into a restaurant or store. That is a struggle these days, one which I am losing and may have to give up!

I also would not have, with Charlie present, expressed the huge sadness that I feel seeing his wonderful mind slip away. It is like losing a little bit of Charlie each day. I read a book, LOVING SOMEONE WHO HAS

Susan and Charlie

DEMENTIA written by Pauline Boss. She also wrote AMBIGUOUS LOSS, the topic of which is somewhat covered in the first one. Good books—I am partial to LOVING SOMEONE . . . Ms. Boss obviously has personal experience with being a caregiver of a person with dementia—someone close to her. When she explained about ambiguous loss, it really hit me. She explained what I and, I am sure, all caregivers (those who truly care for the person for which they care) experience. It is hard. While, like Charlie, I do not choose to dwell on this, it is there—always. While I have expressed to Charlie how sad I feel that he has to deal with this terrible disease, <u>he does not also need to know just how difficult it is for me and our kids</u>.

I will not add to this; mainly I have said what I wanted to say to you. Again, I will be interested in seeing the outcome of your efforts in writing about this really dreadful disease. Realizing that, so far, we do not deal with some of the real horrors that this disease can bring, I am grateful for these days when our life is relatively easy.

Come back to see us again—anytime. Always good to see you. Next time, I might even offer you some iced tea or coffee and, perhaps, even fresh-baked brownies (that were sitting in our kitchen)! Oh well . . . !

Susan

What Helps?

I had dozens of follow-up questions after reading Susan's letter, but most of them could be summed up by "what helps?" She replied:

> Unlike many others dealing with this disease, Charlie and I are blessed with a really wonderful support group of family and friends. I cannot imagine being without them. I have a couple of like-a-sister cousins who live away from here but are great at just being in touch. Everyone else is here, close by, and they are available to help us in any way we need—and they have. Of course, just being with them is a "spirit raiser."

We have a superb primary care physician who works at caring for me and Charlie both. He is honest and supportive; he answers questions and is encouraging. He also referred us to the Pat Summit Clinic at UT Med Center. The neurologist we see there is very kind; he also is very honest. He offers clear explanations and answers all of my questions. When we go, I take a sheet of questions and comments for him to read before he sees us. He says it is helpful and he responds to everything I put on that sheet.

Another help for me is books. The ones that have been the most helpful to me are: *36 Hour Day* (Nancy L. Mace and Peter V. Rabins), *Loving Someone Who Has Dementia* (Pauline Boss) and *Ambiguous Love: Learning to Live with Unresolved Grief* (Pauline Boss).

My main help comes from my faith. Truly, I have no idea how people manage problems—or life in general—without faith. I am grateful for it. God touches me in many ways—as you know . . . through people, through books, through music, through sermons, and, especially, through simple feelings that I have and know they are a reminder that I am never alone and that I am, therefore, strong. I pray a lot; but even on those days when it is hard to pray, I know He gets it. I have tried to learn to ". . . be still and know . . ."

Conclusion

Of all the words I might have heard from Charlie and Susan, "sorry" wasn't one of them. Turns out that "sorry" isn't just another word for the Smith family.

It's been a tradition for several generations of this family to play the board game *Sorry*. Susan played it as a child with her siblings and cousins and mother. She, in turn, taught her children how to play, which they still do. Now their children have learned.

The game board that was used more than sixty years ago has been retired and now hangs on the wall in the kitchen. The Smiths

Susan and Charlie

have a new board, and they like to say that sorry isn't said too often in their family—but that it is played very well.

Sorry may be a paradigm for understanding dementia's effect on a family. Similar to *Parcheesi*, it is a game involving pawns, a board, an altered deck of cards, and a home-zone. The object is to get all of your pawns across the board into the home-zone. The first player to get all of their pawns home wins.

At the beginning of each turn, a player draws a card which tells that player what to do. It might be that the player can move a pawn two steps forward, or he might have to move ten steps backward. There is very little strategy involved as the action is determined entirely by the cards that are drawn.

The best players do influence the game when the opportunity arises (like bumping another player's pawn), but mostly they enjoy the game as it unfolds, one turn at a time. It is the journey they embrace. The cards they draw dictate victory or defeat, and the game goes on and every movement is celebrated or jeered.

In spite of the medical community's best efforts, no one can yet predict who will develop dementia. One day a card might be turned over—and guess what? You have it. Or your spouse. Or a parent. What will everyone say? Sorry! And then the game begins. How do you deal with the cards you draw? The next few chapters will help you influence what comes next. Your journey will not be easy. In fact, it may be the most difficult thing you have ever done. But it will not be devoid of love and grace, either. How you walk it—and who you walk it with—will greatly determine where it takes you.

2

Causes of Dementia

> The advantage of a bad memory is that one enjoys several times
> the same good things for the first time.
> —FRIEDRICH NIETZSCHE

As I met with the chairperson of an associate pastor nominating committee over lunch to discuss my candidacy for their position, I lightheartedly asked what the "unwritten" job description was, thinking there might be some minor congregational issue she would reveal. To my amazement, she responded, "To help the senior pastor retire." It turned out that the senior pastor had been in a horseback riding accident which resulted in a brain injury so traumatic that after surgery he had spent months in rehab learning how to talk and walk again. His recovery had been remarkable, but he was not unscathed. He was an "issue," and for some in the congregation, it was anything but minor.

"Dementia" is the term used to indicate a certain type of brain impairment. It means the brain is damaged, that something is interfering with the ability of brain cells to communicate with each other. Alzheimer's disease is the most common cause of dementia, but it is hardly the only one. Obviously, hitting one's head

Causes of Dementia

after falling off a horse can cause a brain injury. Creutzfeldt-Jakob disease, Huntington's disease, and Parkinson's disease all affect the brain, too. In fact, there are more than a dozen causes of dementia. Some dementias are progressive, others actually may be reversed. All are a concern to family members, congregations, and communities of support, and all are devastating to the patient.

Dementia-Like Conditions and Illnesses

Early in my first pastorate I was asked to see an elderly church member in the hospital who was experiencing difficulty. She was addled and hallucinating. She did not know who I was or where she was. She spoke to her deceased husband; fretted over her children as if they were still infants; bickered with her long-dead mother. Those of us who visited her compared notes and realized there was something odd about her condition. It had come upon her suddenly. One day she was fine, then she didn't feel well, then she was out of touch with reality.

I was totally shocked when I entered her room a few days later and was greeted by name! She went home that same week. Dementia-like symptoms can result from fever or as a side effect from infection. I have seen this over and over again: conditions that compromise the immune system can produce the kind of symptoms we associate with dementia. It is important to remember this. There is enough anxiety about dementia as it is without jumping to conclusions and adding fuel to the fire.

Other things that can bring about dementia-like symptoms include metabolic problems, such as too little sugar in the bloodstream, or too much sodium or calcium. Nutritional deficiencies (not enough B-6 or B-12), reactions to medications (drug interactions), and a subdural hematoma may all generate dementia-like behaviors.

A man I knew in West Virginia was periodically admitted to the psychiatric unit of the local hospital with dementia-like symptoms. Each time, he was pumped full of fluids, given vitamin B-1, his condition improved, and he was released. Eventually I realized that in his case, chronic alcoholism carried its own set of dementia-like symptoms.

Exposure to pesticides, lead poisoning, brain tumors, and a condition known as anoxia—when organ tissues aren't getting enough oxygen—may all result in memory problems or confusion.

Signs and Symptoms

When thinking about dementia, a helpful definition found on the Mayo Clinic website is this: dementia is "a group of symptoms affecting memory, and cognitive and social abilities severely enough to interfere with daily functioning."[1] It goes on to add that a person must have "problems with at least two brain functions, such as memory loss and impaired judgment or language, and the inability to perform some daily activities" before dementia is suspected.[2] A person with dementia experiences both cognitive and psychological changes. Cognitive changes include memory loss, difficulty communicating or finding words, problems with disorientation, and impaired motor skills. Psychological changes might be inappropriate behavior, paranoia, or hallucinations.

Years ago, one of the nicest women I have known (I was named after her husband) was placed in a nursing home because she was unable to care for herself. For decades, she had been a church school teacher and a mainstay at the local health clinic. As her condition deteriorated, this lovely person began to hiss and spit at anyone who approached her. She became the antithesis of her previous self. No wonder we fear dementia for ourselves and for those we love!

In addition to cognitive and psychological changes, problems with complex tasks, difficulty with planning and organizing, personality changes, continually misplacing items, and agitation over minor issues may all indicate dementia.

1. Mayo Clinic, "Dementia," https://www.mayoclinic.org/diseases-conditions/dementia/symptoms-causes/syc-20352013.

2. Mayo Clinic, "Dementia," https://www.mayoclinic.org/diseases-conditions/dementia/symptoms-causes/syc-20352013.

Causes of Dementia

My first encounter with a person actually diagnosed with Alzheimer's disease was a woman in her late sixties who began having problems paying her bills. I sat at her kitchen table with her one afternoon trying to help her balance her checkbook. In frustration, she exclaimed: "I know I am supposed to subtract, but I just can't do it!"

A retired attorney began stopping by our church office when he would become disoriented and ask for directions. He was a polite, easy-going man, but as his condition progressed, his personality changed. One day he told our receptionist (who was working on a master's degree in political science in the evenings) that she was barely capable of doing her job at the church and that she wouldn't even be able to greet people as they entered a certain "big box" department store nearby. This out-of-character insult led me to telephone his wife to ask if something was amiss.

Traumatic Brain Injury

One of the things the senior pastor who fell off his horse said whenever he did not like something one of his staff was doing was, "I have suffered a severe brain injury—what's your excuse?" Of course, there was no excuse: neither was there any arguing about it! We learned the awful truth that an injured brain is a damaged brain, and that emotional health is often damaged, too. His mood swings were breathtaking!

Physicians categorize brain injuries as either mild, moderate or severe. Mild traumatic brain injury, also known as a concussion, either doesn't knock you out or does so for thirty minutes or less. Moderate traumatic brain injury causes unconsciousness lasting more than thirty minutes. Severe traumatic brain injury knocks you out for more than twenty-four hours. The symptoms of all three are similar, but the more severe the injury, the more serious and longer-lasting they are.

What are the symptoms of such injuries? They can range from headache, nausea, and dizziness, for a mild case, to convulsions, confusion, and agitation for a severe one. Symptoms usually appear at the time of the injury or soon afterwards, but sometimes may not develop for days or even weeks. Patients report ringing in the ears, blurred vision, sensitivity to light or sound, and changes in sleep patterns. Mood swings, depression, an inability to concentrate, slurred speech, combativeness, memory loss, and anxiety are not uncommon.

One Sunday in worship I was sitting behind the senior pastor when he lost his place while reading his sermon. A long mid-sentence pause ensued. He stuttered. Then he stammered a bit. I finally stood up, peered over his shoulder, found where he had left off, and pointed it out to him. He continued on as if nothing had happened and concluded a fine effort. However, he later angrily confronted me for "showing him up in front of the congregation."

I mentioned this later to one of our elders who said that when the senior pastor got "stuck" in a sermon like that, everyone in the congregation mentally tried to finish the sentence for him!

Once in a staff meeting he became so agitated that he began to tremble. He held on to the edge of the conference table and shook and shook. To save him from embarrassment, I asked everyone but the other associate pastor to leave the room. I then sat down beside him and asked what was going on. He could only grit his teeth and utter: "I can't stop!"

No one who has not experienced a traumatic brain injury can possibly understand how it affects one. Families and congregations need to remember that the effect on the patient's immediate caregiver is every bit as profound as the effect on the patient. For a spouse or a partner (or a coworker), the loved one may literally never be the same person again.

A brain injury doesn't have to happen in as dramatic a fashion as falling off a horse. There's a reason why both children and adults need to wear helmets while biking. Boxers have long been known to suffer from "dementia pugilistica," and we are just now beginning to take seriously the long-term damage that can be done by contact sports like football and soccer.

Causes of Dementia

Aphasia, Frontotemporal Dementia, and Corticobasal Degeneration

Aphasia is a condition that robs one of the ability to communicate. Speech becomes more and more difficult. Even the ability to read is eventually impaired. While aphasia typically occurs after a stroke or a head injury, it can also come on gradually from a slow-growing brain tumor or from some other disease process. In the last congregation I served, two men suffered from aphasia due to rare but related illnesses.

The first was a retired defense attorney, a voracious reader with an expansive vocabulary. His friends (my wife included) teased that he was never satisfied with a "five-cent word" when a "ten-cent one" would do. He loved telling stories. He himself first noticed he was having difficulty finding just the right words to say in court, which eventually prompted his retirement. As time went on, the rest of us began to notice his struggles with self-expression. We began to feel the same thing we had with our senior pastor—the urge to finish his sentences for him! For a while, he would write to us on an iPad that he carried around, but eventually manipulating that device became too frustrating for him.

His aphasia, formally diagnosed as primary progressive aphasia, came on gradually and was not the result of a brain injury or stroke. Test after test failed to discover any direct cause for his condition, but primary progressive aphasia is one of the conditions lumped together in what is called frontotemporal dementia (FTD). Sadly, he entered into a silent, lonely place he was never able to come out of, and we weren't able to enter into it with him. After his death I asked his wife if she was getting used to being alone. She replied that she had been alone for months, even while he was still alive.

The second member of our congregation to suffer from aphasia was a successful businessman, an engineer, a hunter, a fisherman, also an avid reader, a church school leader, and the family event planner. His diagnosis was eventually determined to be corticobasal degeneration (CBD).

His problem was first noticed when photographs taken at an anniversary dinner revealed what his daughter called "a vague look." His coordination began to slip, then his ability to negotiate spacial relationships. His wife recalled that he once tried to open the mailbox but reached out his arm a good two feet short of it. He stopped driving, gave up counting the offering at church, and was unable to plan vacations.

CBD symptoms typically begin in people from fifty to seventy years of age, and CBD is classified as one of the "Parkinson-plus syndromes" (a group of diseases that feature the classic Parkinson's symptoms of tremors, rigidity, poor balance, etc.). Over a period of four years, this vital, energetic man went from being the one person every member of his family depended upon to being completely unable to move or even talk!

These men suffered from diseases characterized by the degeneration of nerve cells in the frontal and temporal lobes of the brain, on the one hand, and of the cerebral cortex and basal ganglia, on the other. Would that more was known about these conditions!

Concluding Comments

Dr. Monica Crane, founder of the Genesis Neuroscience Clinic in Knoxville, Tennessee, has a special interest in frontotemporal dementia. She says its symptoms can be more subtle than those of other dementias and that it is often misdiagnosed as depression or some other mental illness. She notes changes in personality, personal hygiene or appetite (such as overeating), loss of motivation, lack of empathy for others, and impaired judgment.[3]

Unfortunately, not only are the initial symptoms of FTD easily overlooked or misdiagnosed; so is the onset of nearly every other dementia. Perhaps this is the way it is meant to be: by the time one's symptoms are noticed by enough people, their seriousness cannot be ignored. A great deal of grieving is involved in

---

3. She is interviewed in a helpful YouTube video: Dr. Bob Show HD Archives, "'Frontotemporal Dementia' with Dr. Monica Crane."

coming to terms with dementia, on the part of the patient as well as the family.

3

The Big Three Causes

> Remembrance of things past is not necessarily
> the remembrance of things as they were.
> —MARCEL PROUST

THE THREE MAJOR CAUSES of dementia—accounting for nearly two-thirds of all cases—are Alzheimer's disease, vascular dementia, and dementia with Lewy bodies. Let's take them in reverse order, after which we will review what researchers call "mixed diagnoses" as well as one relatively new type of dementia, observed only in the past decade or so.

Lewy Body Dementia

Experts estimate that dementia with Lewy bodies, or Lewy body dementia (LBD), accounts for 10 to 25 percent of all dementias. Named after Frederick Lewy, a neurologist who worked with Alois Alzheimer (yes, that Alzheimer!) in the early 1900s, LBD is characterized by microscopic deposits of a protein, alpha-synuclein,

The Big Three Causes

throughout the brain. These are the "bodies" of LBD, and their presence is linked to the destruction of the brain cells around them.

Lewy bodies are found in other brain disorders, too, including Parkinson's disease. Many people with Parkinson's eventually develop problems with thinking and reasoning, and many people with LBD experience problems with movement. For this reason, LBD is sometimes considered an "umbrella" term that applies to both conditions.

While dementia is the primary symptom of LBD, patients and caregivers report changes in the ability to concentrate, hallucinations, bodily stiffness or rigidity, sleep disorders, dizziness, and a whole host of other issues.

The authors of *Aging Together* report that "Those who have LBD may fluctuate in cognitive function, attention, and alertness in cycles that last hours, days, weeks, or months."[1] Little wonder that LBD is referred to as a "multi-system disease" that requires "a comprehensive treatment approach with a collaborative team of physicians from varying specialties."[2]

The autopsy of actor Robin Williams indicated that he was suffering from LBD. According to other reports, he was being treated for Parkinson's disease at the time of his death as well, which gives credence to the difficulty in diagnosing this illness. Disc jockey Casey Kasem, too, was incorrectly diagnosed as having an advanced form of Parkinson's disease before it was discovered that he had LBD.

One complication of this is that the medications that treat the motor symptoms of Parkinson's disease can increase risk-taking behaviors and may even stimulate hallucinations and delusions. Mr. Williams experienced numerous symptoms. His wife has been quoted as saying, "It was not depression that killed Robin. Depression was one of let's call it 50 symptoms and it was a small one."[3]

---

1. McFadden and McFadden, *Aging Together*, 23.
2. Whitworth and Whitworth, *A Caregiver's Guide*, 4.
3. Welsh, "Robin Williams' Widow," lines 17–18.

Unfortunately, there is no cure. The disease process typically lasts from three to eight years after the onset of specific symptoms, but it may continue in an individual for much longer than that.

Vascular Dementia

Vascular dementia (VaD) is a term describing problems with reasoning, planning, judgment, memory, and other thought processes caused by brain damage from impaired blood flow to your brain. It is also known as multi-infarct dementia (MID) and vascular cognitive impairment (VCI).

It isn't a disease, exactly, but may be a consequence of something else. For instance, you can develop vascular dementia if a stroke blocks an artery in your brain. It can also be caused by conditions that damage blood vessels and reduce circulation, such as high blood pressure, high cholesterol, and smoking. Possibly as much as 20 percent of all dementias fall into this category.

A woman in our congregation who was outgoing, talkative, and energetic suffered a stroke. Now she barely interacts with others at all. Another woman was an aging marvel to all who knew her: she neither acted nor thought "her age." But after a fall in which she broke her hip—and the resultant surgery—she was no longer her "pre-fall" self. In both cases, vascular dementia is to blame.

As vascular dementia is the second leading cause of dementia in the United States, it is worth taking note of what is known about its risk factors, which are similar to those of heart disease and stroke: increased age, high blood pressure, high cholesterol levels, atherosclerosis, diabetes, smoking, and atrial fibrillation. In addition, if you have had a heart attack or a stroke, you are at an increased risk for vascular dementia.

Given the above, treatment for vascular dementia invariably involves lifestyle changes. Exercise classes held in assisted living facilities do more than simply keep a resident moving! During one of our annual stewardship campaigns one woman repeatedly turned in a pledge card. Our treasurer would dutifully inform her that she had already done so, and a few days later another one would arrive. This woman's short-term memory problems were our first clue that she was dealing with what was eventually diagnosed as vascular dementia.

Alzheimer's Disease

The National Institute on Aging has produced a startling "fact sheet" on Alzheimer's disease (AD). The first sentence reads: "Alzheimer's disease is an irreversible, progressive brain disorder that slowly destroys memory and thinking skills, and eventually the ability to carry out the simplest tasks."[4] It is the most common cause of dementia among older adults, responsible for anywhere from 50 per cent to 70 per cent of all dementias.

It is common and it is deadly. Researchers are beginning to suspect that Alzheimer's disease has been under-reported for years. Updated estimates are that it may be the underlying cause of more than five hundred thousand deaths each year. If this is correct, Alzheimer's disease does not rank sixth, as reported on the Alzheimer's Association's website, but third among causes of death for older adults, behind heart disease and cancer. Today there are more than five million Americans suffering with Alzheimer's. The number of people with the disease doubles every five years beyond age sixty-five. By 2050 there will be fourteen million of us with this disease.

Unfortunately, it isn't just older adults that worry about Alzheimer's. Tennessee Lady Vol basketball fans were stunned in August 2011 to learn that Coach Pat Summitt had been diagnosed with early-onset Alzheimer's disease. She was fifty-nine years old. Although she coached her team for one more year, she was clearly not herself.

Early-onset Alzheimer's is Alzheimer's disease in people sixty-five years of age or younger. It has been known to develop as early as a person's thirties, but this is mercifully rare. It is estimated that about 5 percent of all Alzheimer's patients have early-onset,

---

4. https://www.nia.nih.gov/health/alzheimers-disease-fact-sheet.

and that many of these have a family history of dementia. Pat Summitt's grandmother died with early-onset dementia.

First described in 1906 by Dr. Alois Alzheimer in Munich, Germany, AD is characterized by abnormal "plaques and tangles" in the brain. Brain "shrinkage" also occurs, and connections between nerve cells are lost.

Many professionals describe AD as progressing in three general stages (mild, moderate, and severe), with some proposing seven stages ranging from "no impairment" to "very severe decline."[5] But no matter what it is referred to when diagnosed, the symptoms of Alzheimer's disease are the same. Below are questions based on the Alzheimer's Association's document "Know the 10 Signs."

1. Do you have memory loss that disrupts your daily life?
2. Do you have challenges in planning or solving problems?
3. Do you have difficulty completing familiar tasks at home, or at work, or at leisure?
4. Do you ever get confused about time or place?
5. Do you ever have trouble understanding visual images and spatial relationships?
6. Do have problems finding the right words to say or write?
7. Do you misplace things and have trouble retracing your steps?
8. Do you have increasingly poor judgement?
9. Have you withdrawn from work or social activities?
10. Has your personality or general mood changed?[6]

Unfortunately, print news media and the internet are filled with articles warning about "subtle early warning signs of dementia," "memory slips portend Alzheimer's," "recognizing early signs of dementia," and so on. Thoughts of dementia are scary enough without such a depressing bombardment of information.

---

5. "What Are the 7 Stages of Alzheimer's Disease?" https://www.alzheimers.net/stages-of-alzheimers-disease/.

6. Based on "Know the 10 Signs" on alz.org.

The Big Three Causes

The fact is that any of us, for a variety of reasons not related to dementia, can answer "yes" on any given day to one or more of the questions asked above. Who hasn't forgotten to turn off the lights? Or shut the garage door? Still, it is important to pay attention to such things. Tyler Summitt, Pat Summitt's son, said about his mother's early symptoms, "She lost her keys three times a day instead of once."[7] It is all about behaviors that are out of character.

About being out of character: once one of our sweetest older members was in worship when an interim pastor preached his final service. As he began to talk about packing up and leaving—and seemed to be taking his time about it—she began to urge him to do so: "Go ahead and leave. Just leave. Why doesn't he leave?" She repeated this louder and louder. Her daughter was mortified, but the rest of us couldn't help but smile as she verbalized what many of us were thinking!

Alas, there is no cure for Alzheimer's disease. The disease process generally lasts anywhere from four to eight years after diagnosis, although some persons are thought to have had the disease for as long as twenty years.[8]

Mixed Dementias

Unsurprisingly, dementias do not exist in a vacuum. A "type" of dementia that physicians are becoming increasingly aware of is mixed dementia! The Alzheimer's Association defines mixed dementia as "a condition in which abnormalities characteristic of more than one type of dementia occur simultaneously."[9] For instance, the kind of "plaques and tangles" associated with Alzheimer's disease have been found in brain autopsies along with the kind of blood vessel problems found in Vascular Dementia.

---

7. Jenkins, "Pat Summitt."

8. "Overview of Disease Progression," https://www.alz.org/alzheimers-dementia/stages.

9. "Mixed Dementia," https://www.alz.org/alzheimers-dementia/what-is-dementia/types-of-dementia/mixed-dementia.

In fact, some researchers are now saying that Alzheimer's rarely occurs alone![10]

A study conducted by the Rush Alzheimer's Disease Center and the Rush Institute for Healthy Aging in Chicago concluded that "more than 50 percent of those whose brains met pathological criteria for Alzheimer's had pathologic evidence of one or more coexisting dementias."[11] One implication of this is that since not all medication prescribed for one type of dementia is helpful for all types, health care professionals may be working at cross-purposes when a mixed diagnosis exists.

Obviously, the impact of multiple dementias on the brain can be much more traumatic that one type alone. All the more reason to be supportive of those struggling with dementia, as the disease process may be quicker and more profound with mixed dementias than with a solitary type of dementia.

HIV Dementia

Sadly enough, new causes of dementia are still being discovered. More, probably, are yet unknown. One of the latest is HIV dementia, also known as AIDS dementia complex (ADC).

This type of dementia is caused by an HIV infection in the tissue of the brain, but the exact process of this dementia's development is not clear. The symptoms, however, are depressingly familiar: progressive memory loss, decreased ability to concentrate, a general slowing of cognitive processes, and mood disorders. Motor dysfunction may also be present.

It is estimated that between 20 percent and 35 percent of all HIV-positive people will eventually develop some symptoms of ADC, but this is thought to be so only for persons who have been HIV infected for years and years.

---

10. "What is Mixed Dementia?" https://www.nia.nih.gov/health/what-mixed-dementia-causes-and-diagnosis.

11. "Mixed Dementia," https://www.alz.org/alzheimers-dementia/what-is-dementia/types-of-dementia/mixed-dementia.

Decades ago I would not have been hopeful that many congregations could prove helpful to a person dealing with ADC. I no longer think this. As time has gone on, the stigma of AIDS has dissipated as we have seen the human face of the suffering it causes. This has freed us from the judgments that might have previously paralyzed our compassion. No one, for any reason, should deal with dementia alone.

Conclusion

As disquieting as dementias are, that fact that most of them are slow and progressive may be what C. S. Lewis called "a severe mercy." There is time to provide care; time to talk; time to heal old wounds. And there is still time to live. The congregations I have served have been immeasurably enriched by the participation of members diagnosed with some type of dementia.

The retired attorney who berated our receptionist had been on drug therapy for Alzheimer's disease for nearly six years before we caught on to his condition. He had an active, volunteer-filled life up until shortly before he died.

A woman in a nursing home in Greenup, Kentucky, whom I often visited talked incessantly, but pleasantly, about her childhood, often mistaking me for the "boy who lived down the street." Her last years were wrapped in a mantle of comforting remembrance.

A man with dementia attends a Bible study I lead. He never offers a prayer, and hardly ever comments on a text we've read, but he is a faithful, interested member. When we ask what he has done the past week, he always says the same thing: "Whatever my wife tells me to do!"

Another woman, whose family was able to keep her in their various homes almost until the end, produced a steady stream of antics and comments to remember her by. For instance, whenever she thought she was going to be moved from one location to another, she would get up in the middle of the night and empty all the kitchen cabinets. And while watching the retirement tribute for

Do Not Cast Me Away

Pat Summit on television, she turned to her granddaughters and exclaimed, "No one made a fuss over me when I lost my mind!"

4

Memory

> Memory is necessary not simply for recollection,
> but also for cognition and perception.
> —PAULA FREDRIKSEN

THE ONE THING ALL forms of dementia have in common is the impairment of memory. More than any other kind of disability or injury, memory loss strikes at the heart of what it means to be human. It is what makes dementia so frightening. Time and time again I have heard parishioners say something like, "I'd rather have cancer than Alzheimer's—I'd die sooner, but at least I'd keep my mind." What are we if not beings with the ability to think and to remember? Of course, some cancers take our memories, but the point is that having a mind, being able to think, to remember, to process thoughts and feelings, enables us to bridge the gap between ourselves and others. Without this ability are we still who we once were? Without this ability are we still human?

What Is Memory?

Joshua Foer declared in *Moonwalking with Einstein* that "once upon a time, memory was at the root of all culture, but over the thirty millennia since humans began painting their memories on cave walls, we've gradually supplanted our own natural memory with a vast superstructure of external memory aids—a process that has sped up exponentially in recent years."[1] But what Foer wonders is this:

> As our culture has transformed from one that was fundamentally based on internal memories to one that is fundamentally based on memories stored outside the brain, what are the implications for ourselves and for our society? What we've gained is indisputable. But what have we traded away? What does it mean that we've lost our memory?[2]

Simply stated, memory is the process in which information is encoded, stored, and retrieved. Dementia inhibits all three of these aspects of memory, but the degree to which it affects each varies with differing diagnoses and from individual to individual. Just because a parishioner cannot retrieve your name, for example, does not mean he or she does not know who you are!

Augustine on Memory

Christian theology has a long history of pondering memory. In AD 397, St. Augustine, then bishop of Hippo (in what is now Algeria), published his autobiography, which he entitled (in Latin) *Confessions in Thirteen Books*. Composed in three parts—past, present, and future—it is the section on the present that contains his thoughts on the role of memory in the heart's ascent to God.

Early in *Confessions* Augustine recites his well-known prayer, "You have made us for yourself, and our hearts are restless, until

---

1. Foer, *Moonwalking with Einstein*, 18.
2. Foer, *Moonwalking with Einstein*, 19.

Memory

they can find rest in you."³ What he does not reveal until later is that the restlessness of the heart of which he speaks is a product of memory. Unable to find God by way of the senses, or through external experiences, Augustine concludes that the way to God is inward, by searching the mind.

He begins book 10 with an exploration of different types of memory and marvels at how they work. "Great is this force of memory, excessive great, O my God; a large and boundless chamber! Who ever sounded the bottom thereof? Yet is this a power of mine, and belongs unto my nature; nor do I myself comprehend all that I am."⁴

Eventually restlessness reappears as the universal pursuit of happiness (which I take to be "meaning" or "purpose"). Marveling that we can even "remember forgetfulness" Augustine concludes that since all of us are searching for meaning for our lives, we must have some memory of it, else we would not be searching at all.⁵

Memory, therefore, must contain *a priori* knowledge that allows the mind to comprehend God, once truly encountered. How else would we recognize God unless some awareness of God were not already in our memories?

Sadly, Augustine evidently never considered a person whose memory was demented. What is that person's relationship to God? Is an awareness of God still present? Can God still be recognized?

How Memory Works

As I understand it, memory works something like this. Encoding, the first step in creating a memory, begins with perception. Our senses register colors, shapes, sounds, odors, and textures. This data is integrated into one single experience in the hippocampus of our brains. The frontal cortex of the brain gets involved and somehow determines if it is an experience worth remembering. If

---

3. Augustine, *Confessions*, I.i.1.
4. Augustine, *Confessions*, X.viii.15.
5. Augustine, *Confessions*, X.x.17.

so, the memory is stored in various places throughout the brain. Once the information is stored, it can be retrieved.

This process is accomplished by electrical pulses that flow from nerve cells across connecting points (synapses) to other nerve cells by means of chemical messengers called neurotransmitters. As one cell signals to another, the synapse between them grows stronger. Conversely, if a cell rarely signals to an adjacent cell, the synapse between them grows weaker. A typical brain is thought to have about one hundred trillion synapses, and our memories are stored and retrieved along the circuits created between them.

A person with dementia has fewer and fewer synapses as the disease progresses. When an Alzheimer's patient says he or she can't remember something, it may be that the synapses between brain cells necessary for that specific remembrance no longer exist. It is literally true: the memory cannot be retrieved. It is cruel to try to "force" a person with dementia to remember something that may be no longer there.

Volf on Memory

While St. Augustine used his understanding of memory as a proof for the existence of God, theologian Miroslav Volf took a very different tack on memory. Volf, the Henry B. Wright Professor of Theology at Yale Divinity School, is a prolific author. Perhaps his most controversial book is entitled *The End of Memory*. Ben Myers posted the following summation of it on the website Faith and Theology.

> Volf weaves his theological and psychological analysis around an unsettling set of memories from his own past. In the communist Yugoslavia of the early 1980s, Volf's theological studies were interrupted by a summons to compulsory military service. As a Christian married to an American, an advocate of non-violence, and an expert on Marxist socialism, Volf was perceived to be an opponent of the Yugoslavian communist regime. He was thus forced to endure a protracted period of interrogation

Memory

under the military police (his interrogator is described throughout the book as "Captain G.")

Long after these events, Volf has remained haunted by the memories of his interrogation. Thus the central question of this book: how do we "remember rightly"? This was a question of great importance for Volf himself, since "My soul was at stake in the way I remembered Captain G." (p. 17). So what does it mean to remember rightly? If we are followers of Jesus Christ, we must be committed to remembrance *as reconciliation*—to memory as "a bridge between adversaries instead of a deep and dark ravine that separates them" (p. 35).[6]

My guess is that most Alzheimer's patients would give anything for the ability to sort out "remembering rightly" from "remembering wrongly." Still, it must be admitted that for some people, the forgetfulness of dementia may be a release from the torment of traumatic memories. But the question still remains: what of a person whose memory is impaired by disease? Can such a person remember "rightly"? Is reconciliation a possibility without remembrance?

Sensory vs. Short-Term vs. Long-Term

A common model for understanding memory was developed by Richard Atkinson and Richard Shiffrin in 1968.[7] They proposed three "stages" of a memory process that progresses from sensory to short-term to long-term memory.

Sensory memory is the ability to retain impressions of sensory information after the original stimuli have ended, even if only for a few seconds. When we see something and remember what it looked like with only a cursory glance, we have experienced sensory memory.

---

6. Myers, "Miroslav Volf."
7. McLeod, "Multi Store Model of Memory."

Short-term memory is "the brain's Post-it note."[8] This is the ability to remember and process information at the same time. Short-term memory holds a small amount of information in mind in an active state for a short period of time, perhaps a minute or so.

Long-term memory, as the term suggests, stores information over an extended period of time. Despite the impression that we forget things we wish to remember, research indicates that long-term memory actually decays very little over time. We can store a seemingly unlimited amount of information almost indefinitely.

Short-term memories become lodged in our long-term memory through a process of "rehearsal" and "meaningful association." Whereas short-term memory relies on an "acoustic" and "visual" code for storing information, long-term memory encodes information "semantically," which is what is meant by meaningful association.[9]

As mentioned earlier, whenever something is learned, circuits of nerve cells in the brain are created. These neurons communicate with one another through junctions called synapses. Through a process that involves the creation of proteins within the neurons, and the chemical transfer of neurotransmitters across synapse gaps to receptors in the adjacent nerve cells, the strength of these circuits of neurons in the brain is reinforced. With repeated use, the efficiency of these synapse connections increases.

Our knowledge of memory is finally moving beyond models. Scientists now know that new information enters the brain through the entorhinal cortex and then is relayed to the hippocampus for short-term memory storage. As nerve cells in the entorhinal cortex begin dying, the connection to the hippocampus is gradually eroded and finally lost. The entorhinal cortex is the first part of the brain to be affected by Alzheimer's, which is why short-term memory loss is such an important indicator of possible disease.

---

8. McLeod, "Multi Store Model of Memory."
9. McLeod, "Multi Store Model of Memory."

Memory

Created in the Image of God

In various places the Bible affirms that humanity was created in the image of God, but without defining what that means (see Gen 1:26–27; Ps 8; Heb 2:5–9). For Judaism, it cannot mean that we are made in the physical image of God, because God is incorporeal and has no physical appearance. Rashi explained that we are like God in that we have the ability to understand and discern.[10] Maimonides taught that by using our intellect we are able to perceive things without the use of our physical senses, which is what makes us like God, who also perceives without having physical senses.[11]

Augustine, whose writings have been previously mentioned, used a trinitarian formula to describe the image of God as a combination of "memory, intellect, and will."[12] The Reformers thought the image of God in humanity was much more subtle than intellect or rationality, and that whatever it was it had been marred or even destroyed by human sin.[13]

More recent theologians like Karl Barth argue that it is our ability to establish and maintain complex and intricate relationships that makes us like God.[14] Calvin Butts, pastor of Abyssinian Baptist Church in New York City, argued at a 2016 conference I attended in Chautauqua, New York, that the image of God in humanity has to do with "self-consciousness, with personality, with the ability to say 'I.'"[15]

None of the above, however, considers what it means to be human and to be unable to function intellectually or rationally or even relationally. Over and over I have heard family members and close friends of a person with dementia say something like, "He just isn't in there anymore," or, "She is just the shell of herself." Nothing disturbs us more than a disease that calls into question

---

10. Rashi, *Commentary on Genesis*, Gen 1:27.
11. "Human Nature," https://www.mechon-mamre.org/jewfaq/human.htm.
12. Augustine, *Confessions*, X.x.18.
13. "The Scots Confession," ch. 3.
14. Barth, *Humanity of God*, 42.
15. Butts, "In the Image of God."

our very humanity. (I worry that someday, as the sheer number of dementia patients increases and as the cost of caring for them rises, a fascist bureaucratic decision might be made that they aren't still human and that appropriate care may be discontinued.)

Conclusion

In Knoxville I visited an elderly member of our church who seemed to have no memory at all. Every conversation I had with him was identical to the previous one. I would say, "Hello, my name is Paul. I am one of the pastors of your church."

He would respond with a surprised look, "You are? I am so glad to see you." Then he would say, "Who are you?"

I would reply, "My name is Paul. I am one of the pastors of your church."

He would repeat, surprised again, "You are? I am so glad to see you . . . Who are you?"

Around and around we went. I tried every verbal trick I knew to break this cycle, but no matter what I said, or how I said it, he always asked, "Who are you?"

The disease process had robbed him of the ability to access his long-term memory, and his short-term memory barely functioned at all. His surprise at meeting someone seemed genuine, but in retrospect, it may have been merely a reflex. Still, he was a lovely man and it was heartbreaking to endure an afternoon with him. He seemed to recognize his wife of sixty-plus years, even though he repeatedly asked who *she* was. Nevertheless, she sat with him every day for several years until he died. When I asked her why she spent so much time with him, she answered, "He would do the same for me." Clearly, even without a working memory, he was still human to her.

5

Assessment

> Nothing can last forever. There isn't any memory, no matter how intense, that doesn't fade out at last.
> —JUAN RULFO

"WE THINK SOMETHING MIGHT be wrong with dad. Would you visit him and see what you think?" My heart sank at hearing this request, because those of us around the church office had just had a conversation about the same thing. Something was wrong with this person's father! But what?

Everyone has memory problems from time to time. (Remember my water sprinkler?) And there are many different things that interfere with cognition: anxiety, medications, fatigue, overwork, trauma, vitamin deficiencies, insomnia, alcoholism, and types of infection are but a few. The question is, how does one reach a determination that trouble remembering something may be a very serious problem?

Self-Assessment

The website of Alzheimer's Reading Room contains information on what it calls "the five best memory tests" for determining if you have dementia or Alzheimer's disease. They are free to anyone with a computer. The first one is called SAGE (Self-Administered Geo-cognitive Examination), a fifteen-question written exam that takes just a few minutes to complete. Developed by Dr. Douglas Scharre, of the Ohio State University Medical Center in Columbus, Ohio, it is designed to evaluate every part of a patient's brain, from language to memory to problem solving.

I downloaded SAGE and took it myself. It asked questions such as: "How far did you get in school?" "Have you had any problems with memory or thinking?" "Do you have balance problems?" "Have you ever had a major stroke?" "Do you have difficulties doing everyday activities due to thinking problems?" and so forth.[1] It asks what today's date is, and to "name" what the pictures of a wreath and a volcano are. There are simple math problems, a drawing test, "connect the dots," and a memory test. The directions encourage those who take the test to allow a primary care physician to see the results. (No answer sheet is provided.)

Drawing a clock by hand is another quick screening tool that can help detect dementia and is one of the components of SAGE. Try it yourself. Draw a clock on a piece of paper. Include the face and put the numbers in the correct positions. Let it show a specific time. This test you can score yourself: one point for a closed circle, one point for properly placed numbers, one point for including all twelve numbers, and one point for properly placed hands. If you find the results disturbing, take them to your physician. (Of course, if a person refuses to draw a clock, that too might signal a problem.)

What's known as the "Mini-Cog" (short for "mini-cognitive") is a three-part diagnostic exam that can be given by one individual to another.[2] First, name three random objects and ask the person

---

1. "SAGE: A Test to Detect Signs of Alzheiemr's and Dementia," https://wexnermedical.osu.edu/brain-spine-neuro/memory-disorders/sage.

2. See mini-cog.com.

Assessment

being tested to repeat them back to you. (If the person cannot repeat the three objects after a few tries, please consult a physician immediately.) If the person can complete this task, move on to the following: ask the person to draw a clock. The clock should have the right shape and correct numbers in the exact order. Then, ask the person to repeat the words/objects from the first part of the test.

I tried to download the fourth of the five recommended self-evaluations, the so-called TYM (Test Your Memory) exam, but the online reply I received said it was given out to professionals only. Besides that, the TYM is designed for people that live in England, and the results have been published in the British Medical Journal.

The final test was the "Dr. Oz Alzheimer's Memory Quiz," which proved to be more of an assessment of what an individual knows about risk factors than anything else. Dr. Oz asks four questions:

1. Do age, gender and family history affect your Alzheimer's risk?
2. A concussion can increase your Alzheimer's risk, true or false?
3. Practicing an "intellectual hobby," like dancing or learning a language, can reduce your risk, true or false?
4. There is a correlation between heart disease and an increased risk for Alzheimer's, true or false?[3]

The material that summarizes each question is this:

> Age, gender and family history are the Alzheimer's risk factors you can't control. After 65, your risk doubles. If you have a first-degree relative, like a parent or sibling, with dementia your risk can double or triple. And lastly, being a woman is a risk factor in itself.
>
> Any serious head injury, including a concussion, puts you at risk for Alzheimer's. The more traumas you have had and the degree of seriousness increases your risk; if you've had 3–4 concussions, your risk can triple or quadruple. Wear a helmet and avoid dangerous lifestyle choices that could put you at risk.

---

3. "Quiz: Do You Know Your Risk for Alzheimer's?" https://www.doctoroz.com/quiz/quiz-do-you-know-your-risk-alzheimers.

Learning can help prevent brain deterioration and stave off Alzheimer's. An adult brain still has the capacity to create new nerve cell connections and build up cognitive reserve and resistance to diseases like Alzheimer's. Activities such a dancing, playing an instrument, or learning a new language can help keep the mind sharp and engaged while fighting the effects of Alzheimer's.

There is a connection. Heart disease and vascular problems can cause blockages that limit blood supply to the brain, and increase your risk for Alzheimer's disease. Living heart healthy and making the right diet and exercise choices can also keep your brain healthy and protect you from a multitude of diseases, including Alzheimer's disease.[4]

Assessment Isn't Easy

I once followed a gerontologist on his rounds at a nursing home and was impressed by two things: how compassionate and at ease he was in speaking with people he knew had advanced dementia, and how guarded most of those he spoke to were about their lives. A cursory conversation—like the kind we pastors have with many of our parishioners—would probably not reveal much, if anything, wrong.

One woman in particular threw me for a loop. She was approximately my age and evinced no visible signs of a problem. She was healthy looking, dressed properly, and seemed to know who we were. We chatted about her life in the assisted living section of the nursing home, about her career as an engineer in a government laboratory, and about her church. Finally, though, the repetitive thinking of someone suffering with dementia emerged: every unit of time she referred to was the same. She had worked in the lab for twenty years. She had been in the nursing home for twenty years. She had been married for twenty years. She had known my

---

4. Formerly on www.doctoroz.com; source has since been changed from print to video.

friend the gerontologist for twenty years. Fuzzy details may be a clue to a problem.

One of the comments made over and over again in the literature about dementia is that at least in the early stages of the disease the person affected with dementia will be able to "pull it together" for brief periods of time in order to hide his or her disability. This is why the child living near the parent who is beginning to have problems is able to "see" the dementia but the child who lives far away and only comes home for short visits does not. Self-assessments and the informed opinions of amateurs are helpful, but professional assessments carry the weight necessary to overcome denial in both patient and family.

Identifying what's going on in a person's head isn't easy. The defense attorney suffering from primary progressive aphasia mentioned in chapter 2 went from a speech therapist to dexterity/balance therapy to a local neurologist to a neurological specialist in another state, and finally to an out-of-state clinic. He never did become the patient of a local neurologist specializing in dementia. There is no one simple test, and early symptoms are similar to those of other conditions, as detailed in previous chapters, so there is plenty of room for error and tremendous need for second opinions. So far, only autopsies provide conclusive evidence.

Recently, a blood test being developed at the Washington University School of Medicine in St. Louis, Missouri, was reported to be 94 percent accurate in finding brain changes related to Alzheimer's disease. It is, however, still years away from being available to the medical community.

Begin with Your General Practitioner

About sixty people gathered in the conference room of a local assisted-living facility to hear one of Chattanooga's neurologists answer whatever questions they might have about dementia. After a few tentative queries, someone asked, "Our family doctor is resisting referring dad to a neurologist. What do you think? Should he see someone like you?"

Without batting an eye the neurologist responded, "I wish I could say 'sure he should'—and drum up business for myself—but it probably isn't necessary. There are only fifteen or so neurologists in the area, which isn't enough to see everyone with dementia anyway. Your family physician is able to diagnose it, and neurologists are available for consults even if we can't see every patient."

It all begins with your family doctor. Not only is he or she the person most likely to confirm your suspicions, he or she is often the gatekeeper to appropriate care, specialized treatment, and insurance benefits. Someone official like your primary care physician has to declare: your father or your mother or you yourself may have dementia.

But even here, there should be a second opinion (or even a third one). Recently, a member of our congregation was told by his longtime family physician that he "had dementia." He was forgetful, his short-term memory was impaired, his personality was muted. It made sense. Then it was discovered that he had had two bouts of influenza back-to-back (which lasted weeks!) followed by several months of insomnia. Once he got his strength back, and regained a healthier sleeping pattern, his "dementia" disappeared.

What a Physician Might Say or Do

The advantage a family physician has over a specialist is a relationship with the patient. Often, a family physician has a longterm relationship with the patient, as well as contacts with other members of the patient's family. Do not feel bad about "going behind" a patient's back with concerns over dementia: doctors are often asked by family or friends to assess a person's cognition "without letting the patient know" he or she has been alerted to a possible problem. (HIPAA permits doctors to disclose information to family when a patient is incapacitated or otherwise unable to consent to the disclosure.)

Dr. Christine Parker, who has a family practice in Chattanooga, routinely asks her patients why she is seeing them. She says it is a "check" on their self-knowledge and self-awareness and is often

Assessment

a segue into a discussion about things other than the "presenting" problem. She says an easy way to begin to address cognition is to ask a patient to name animals. How many types can you name? Healthy people can go on and on; those with dementia stop after just a few.

Once an impairment of some sort is suspected, family physicians have a range of more thorough testing they can administer. Although there are as yet no blood tests for dementia, testing for health issues that can cause symptoms of dementia—anemia, infection, diabetes, kidney disease, liver disease, and thyroid abnormalities—are worth checking for.

Family members will almost certainly be brought in to share their concerns for the patient. Medication may be prescribed, but much of what is commonly used for treating memory has little effect. A referral to a driving testing center may be requested if one exists nearby, but unfortunately only two states—Illinois and New Hampshire—require a road test for an older driver. As far as I've been able to determine, no state has yet taken dementia into account when it comes to driver's licenses.

Dr. Parker told me about an elderly woman whose family was concerned about her driving ability. The woman, of course, did not want to give up driving and assured Dr. Parker that she only drove a few places each week, to the grocery store and the like. Nevertheless, she agreed to go to a local testing center "just to be sure." Fortunately for Chattanooga's public safety, the facility she was sent to began with a physical exam that discovered that not only was she unable to turn her head far enough to avoid blind spots, she was hardly able to press the brake pedal far enough to work well.

The family physician's most valuable role may not be in treating a patient for dementia, but in helping that patient and that patient's family deal with the problems caused by dementia. Also, physicians may have insight into the various facilities for patient care that might come into play as the disease worsens.

Conclusion

Probably nothing so irritates us when thinking about the health of those we love as does the realization that there is very little that can be done to stop or reverse the major causes of dementia. There is no surgery, there are no effective pills. Yet we want to "do" something. We want our loved ones to be able to "do" something: work crossword puzzles, subscribe to internet "brain games," learn a language, play an instrument. Exercise seems to be beneficial, too. Movement is generally healthy, for all parts of the body, including the brain. But even exercise won't stop or reverse the major causes of dementia.

What an effective assessment does is break through our resistance so we can begin to take realistic, responsible steps to deal with an illness—either our own or that of a loved one—that is progressive and may last for years.

6

Kinds of Care

> When I was younger, I could remember anything,
> whether it had happened or not.
> —MARK TWAIN

As a pastor in Huntington, West Virginia, a pianist from my congregation and I would sometimes lead a worship service at a local nursing home. Residents would shuffle in with their walkers in front of them, or enter in their wheelchairs. A few would even be brought into the room in their hospital beds. Most of them would fall asleep as I read Scriptures and led them in prayer.

Some of them would awaken when the piano played. Unfortunately, we didn't often find songs that everyone knew, so our singing was more noise than anything else. And I have to admit that no one woke up during the sermon. But something magical happened when we sang "Amazing Grace." Those lost in the empty cavern of dementia came back—if only for the few verses they sang—as if they had been found. Like a scene from the movie *Awakenings*, life came back into tired faces and blank looks disappeared. I was always saddened to watch when we finished as they gradually became lost again.

I also wondered: where did these people come from? How did they get there? Were they being treated right? Where were their families? And how much does it cost to keep them there? Some facilities seem like warehouses for the elderly. Others are more like hotels, or even health clubs. Sorting out the options is a daunting task.

What Kind of Care Is Available?

A few months ago one of our older members tore a ligament in his elbow, necessitating surgery. His left arm would be out of commission for a while. Normally, this calls for our congregation to deliver a round of home-cooked meals to the family and that was that. But this was different because we knew how difficult it was to get him in and out of his home with both of his arms working properly. A victim of adult-onset polio, we couldn't imagine how he would get home from the hospital, navigate his household stairs, or get to follow-up doctor appointments.

What kind of care could be found for him?

The defense attorney with progressive aphasia lived in a lakefront home with front and back stairs leading to the first floor, a sunken living room, complete with an interior spiral staircase. A woman suffering from dementia that I knew in Ashland, Kentucky, lived alone in a two-story house with the bedrooms on the second floor. I can't tell you how many families I have had conversations with over the years that go something like this: "The house mom and dad live in is a nightmare—there are stairs everywhere, the bedrooms are upstairs and so is the bathroom!"

SeniorAdvisor.com tells me there are thirty-four "memory care" options in the Chattanooga area. A Place for Mom says there are fifty "dementia care facilities" near Chattanooga. SeniorHomes.com lists just seven "memory care facilities" in Chattanooga, with three others in nearby locations. And there are other listings merging Alzheimer's and dementia care. Thanks to the internet, it is much easier to locate help than it used to be. Facilities are trying to cover all the bases! But do they? What constitutes an appropriate

Kinds of Care

place for the care of a person with dementia is not easy to define. Most families are faced with at least three "options" when a loved one has a form of dementia: in-home care (which inevitably includes additional help), some sort of residential care, and a type of specialized facility that is becoming known as memory care.

Perils at Home

Two-thirds of Alzheimer's patients are cared for at home by family members. An amazing 25 percent of caregivers are between the ages of eighteen and thirty-four! It is estimated that six out of ten employees will be caregivers at some point while they are still working.[1] The benefits of this for the patient are obvious. Being in familiar surroundings mitigates some of the confusion that dementia causes. The mere thought of a new place with new things is terrifying for many.

An important initial question though is, whose home? Also, is a spouse or another family member alive and able to provide care, or is the patient alone? Almost without fail, a person in the early stages of Azheimer's wishes to stay in his or her home.[2] Later on, a move to a child's home might be advisable, but initially it is best to stay put. However, common sense "changes" need to be made if at all possible.

For instance, since a person with dementia may have problems with their balance, obvious tripping hazards need to be eliminated, such as throw rugs, electric cords, and low-level furniture. Since confusion and paranoia mark some dementias, safety questions need to be asked. Are there weapons in the home? Guns or knives? What about power tools? Lawn mowers? Chainsaws? And good luck with any electronic gadget that uses a remote control!

If the patient is to remain at home, an assessment needs to be made even if a spouse is there, too. It can be a low-key informal

---

1. Ansberry, "Call to Care for Parents."
2. Howley, "Homecare for a Loved One."

affair conducted by family or friends, or an intentional professional one, but it needs to be done.

I once talked to a gerontologist in Knoxville about an older friend dealing with depression. The gerontologist went to his home and was immediately struck by how dark the interior was. All the windows were closed and the drapes pulled. He walked through the house and opened just enough of them so as to "not be obvious" about it. Later our friend commented to me that he had not realized how gloomy his house had become, and that he felt a little better just from having more light shine into his home. There is always an advantage to an outsider's perspective.

There's no end to the kinds of modifications that can be made to a home. Grab bars for the bathroom, taller toilets, ramps for the steps, hidden turn-off valves for the gas stove, and locks for cabinets containing poisonous or flammable liquids are just a few. The trick, of course, is to know when to make these changes and how to make them in a way that will be accepted by the patient.

Some houses just aren't easily or reasonably "modifiable." One family I know made a deal with their mother, who was increasingly unsteady on her feet: she was allowed to stay in her sprawling four-thousand-square-foot home—alone—on the condition that she not go upstairs to the second story. The staircase was roped off (in a way that the family could tell if she meddled with it) so she was restrained from wandering to the second floor. Eventually she had to leave her home, but she was able to stay there much longer than if they had not negotiated limits she could abide by.

Help at Home

One of our older members, who lives alone in her own home, is able to get to church events because she discovered a "driver" who will take her places. Another woman has "help" eight hours a day, five days a week. A couple, both in their nineties, continues to live in their apartment with the aid of their daughters, who take turns staying with them at night. There seems to be no limit to the kind of "in-home" help being offered these days. One of my grandmother's friends once told me, "America is a great place to grow old in—if you can find the help!"

Only in the early stages of dementia can a person live alone in safety. Once the disease has progressed past the initial stage, if a person is at home it almost always means that a "primary" caregiver is also there. That may be you! Welcome to "the sandwich generation"—those who are sandwiched in between responsibilities to children and grandchildren, on the one hand, and parents, on the other.

Our county is part of the Southeast Tennessee Area Agency on Aging and Disability (AAAD), which takes its mandate from the 1965 Older Americans Act. Its goal is "to advocate for and to strive to achieve a system of services that allows older persons and persons with disabilities the opportunity for an independent and productive lifespan."[3] Grammatical issues with this goal nonwithstanding, among the services AAAD provides are family caregiver support groups, information on protecting your senior from financial exploitation, home delivered meals, homemaker services (light housekeeping, mending, ironing, etc.), health screenings, and more.

As of 2016, an Area Agency on Aging (AAA) was listed in 622 locations throughout the United States, which assures that virtually every caregiver in our country is within reach of some form of help.

Residential Care

According to A Place for Mom, the terms:

> "residential care homes," "adult family homes," "board and care homes," and "personal care homes" are industry terms to describe certain communities and/or facilities. These terms may or may not reflect official state requirements concerning licensing, level of care, and/or the services that are provided.[4]

3. "Older Americans Act." https://www.n4a.org/olderamericansact.
4. https://www.aplaceformom.com/care-homes.

It recommends that when considering a facility, be sure to request to see their state license. Clarification of license type, level of care, and the services that are provided is essential.

For instance, Tennessee residential homes (or a home for the aged) provide room and board and some assistance with personal needs, such as eating and grooming. A resident must be physically and mentally capable of finding a way to safety in the event of an emergency without assistance from someone else.

Such homes for the aged are not staffed nor licensed to provide nursing care. In fact, Tennessee state law prohibits "homes for the aged" from accepting residents who need medical care. They're designed to provide a place where people who are able to care for themselves with little or no help may receive room, board, and personal services. Personal services are defined as help bathing; hair and nail grooming; dressing; laundry; and the self-administration of medications.

Is residential care able to provide for a person with dementia? Maybe. Some places will try. My observation is that by the time most families come to grips with the reality of a loved one's dementia, the time for a residential home has passed. Still, it can be a useful way station on the road to more specialized care.

Thinking about placing mom or dad in a "home" is traumatic. How do you know it is time? Ask yourself some of these questions: Are they finding it more and more difficult to shower and bath, even with help? Have they fallen recently? Has their balance and mobility worsened? Do they forget to take their medication? Do they wander off? Are you worried about their safety? It is a tragedy to be in "denial" about their condition until a major medical emergency forces your hand.

Assisted Living

It is estimated that six out of every ten people with dementia will "wander."[5] Residential homes are not equipped to deal with this.

5. "Wandering," https://www.alz.org/help-support/caregiving/stages-behaviors/wandering.

Neither are most assisted living facilities, which are designed to allow patients to come and go, if able. That's the big question mark for all assisted living facilities: how much assistance is provided?

An organized way to proceed might be to research online and by phone, tour facilities you might be interested in, and dig for more information with finalists. Initial research asks such questions as: Is the location close to shops, doctor's offices, a pharmacy, and other important places? Is the location convenient for family and friends to visit? If the facility is not in your town, are there hotels nearby for when you visit the area? And, what are others saying about this provider?

When you tour a facility some of the things you should consider are: Is there easy parking outside, including handicapped spaces? Is parking provided? Is the building's exterior clean and attractive? Is there a safe area where residents can walk and socialize? Are the common spaces pleasant and appealing? Are hallways well lit and easy to navigate, with handrails and plenty of room for wheelchairs? Are pets allowed? Do residents have private rooms? Are the bathrooms handicap-equipped? Are the rooms personalized? What kind of furniture is allowed? Is there adequate closet and storage space? Are there planned activities? And what about the food?

When you have narrowed your options down to the final few facilities, drop in unexpectedly a time or two, and at different hours. Ask for a copy of a resident bill of rights, survey results from state regulators, and talk to several of the residents. Your pastor or priest probably visits a lot of nursing homes: ask his or her opinion. To put a loved one in an assisted living facility, especially if he or she is unhappy about it, may be an agonizing decision to make, but may simply have to be done.[6]

---

6. A comprehensive list of these and other questions to ask is found on care.com, "Checklist: Questions to Ask When Choosing a Nursing Home," https://www.care.com/c/stories/15707/choosing-nursing-home-questions-to-ask/.

Conclusion

As a pastor, I have been privy to the traumas of dealing with housing for the elderly, and especially with housing those with dementia, more times than I can count. (I started to write "more times than I can remember.") A family therapist once told me to encourage families to "do the math." If taking care of mom or dad overburdens the rest of the family, then who can take care of, or make decisions for, the rest of them?

7

Memory Care

When you remembered to forget, you were remembering.
It was when you forgot to forget that you forgot.

—ANN BRASHARES

IF A RESIDENT IS in good health, is mobile, and can take care of his or her basic needs, an assisted living facility may be adequate for years, even if dementia is slowly eroding the resident's memory.

One of the members of our congregation is a man who was a soldier in World War II, Korea, and in Vietnam. He was a decorated combat veteran who saw time in both German and Chinese concentration camps! He vividly recalls his trials in those camps and can describe his captors and those he was imprisoned with. But, at times, when I visit him, he glares around his room and complains bitterly that his children have taken all his things, as though he should still be in his old home. He is doing well—physically—but his mind is betraying him, making his decline more painful for his family. Still, he is being cared for!

Memory Care

An article by Lisa Esposito says that "memory care has a gentle ring to it, a sense of precious keepsakes highly valued and lovingly tended." It goes on to remind us that "the keepsakes, however, are not trinkets, but our loved ones."[1] In order to deliver on the promises given, a memory care facility has to have much more than secure units and exit alarms in place.

Here are a few of the things she says a top-notch memory care home will offer:

- Staff members trained to understand the needs of those with dementia.
- A low staff to resident ratio (five residents to one caregiver is common).
- Safe spaces for walking about, for activity, indoors and out.
- A range of care, from early-to-moderate to moderate-to-advanced "units."
- The ability to handle aggressive and destructive behaviors.
- A full staff in the evenings and at night (dementia and sleep dysrhythmia go hand in hand).

Esposito's article suggests "signs" of respectful care on the part of the staff:

- Do staff members respond to individuals in a patient, positive and caring way during interactions?
- Do they communicate with residents as adults who can make choices, affording them dignity rather than treating them as infants?
- Is the staff good at redirecting individuals in ways that don't escalate anxiety or anger? For instance, they might take the time to walk on the grounds with a resident who seems eager to leave the building whenever he sees visitors do so.

1. Esposito, "Nursing Home 'Memory Care.'"

- Are the basics of communication the norm? Looking into people's eyes when speaking and using an appropriate volume and tone of voice are as important as ever in memory care.
- Are staff members gentle in assisting a person to move, rather than pushing him or her in a direction?
- Is the staff open to nonverbal communication methods? For instance, using pictures and symbols, such as pictures of food for eating, or of baths and showers, or indoor and outdoor activities, allows people to make day-to-day choices.[2]

Providing all sorts of health care for seniors is a growth industry. Thanks to the Baby Boom generation, approximately ten thousand people in our country reach the age of sixty-five every day, which will continue for the next twenty years![3]

For-Profit vs. Nonprofit Care

No matter where you live, a for-profit memory care facility is nearby. Chances are, it will be one owned by Brookdale Senior Living, the largest operator of senior living communities in the United States. Based in Brentwood, Tennessee, it oversees more than 1,100 "communities" with eighty thousand employees serving one hundred thousand residents. It is not alone: more than 80 percent of senior residential care facilities are private and for-profit, and about 40 percent are part of national chains.

Other for-profits you may come across in your search for an appropriate facility include: Genesis Healthcare, HCR ManorCare, and Holiday Retirement. But Brookdale is by far the largest.

Monthly fees for senior living appear similar for nonprofit and for-profit communities, but they may not account for everything. For instance, some for-profit homes charge extra for services

---

2. Esposito, "Nursing Home 'Memory Care.'"
3. Heimlich, "Baby Boomers Retire."

such as transportation or assistance bathing and dressing.[4] Laundry services are often extra, as well. This brings up a sticky point. I have heard from dozens of families that laundry is problematic, no matter what kind of facility is in question. Either a family member does the "wash" and gets it back to mom or dad (which can be a grueling routine), or they let the facility do it and wonder what happened to the items found to be missing, which is frustrating to say the least.

Presbyterian Senior Living, of Dillsburg, PA, provides an ebook entitled, *Clearing up Differences between Non-Profit and For-Profit Senior Living Organizations*. Admittedly biased toward nonprofit care, PSL declares that nonprofit senior care organizations and for-profit ones are distinguished in significant ways. It declares that nonprofits provide better care because their mission is different and their stakeholders are distinct from those in the for-profit sector.

Here are some of PSL's key points worth considering:

- In general, non-profit communities have higher staffing ratios and a higher number of registered nurses than for-profit communities.
- Non-profit communities more often rely on acuity-based staffing models, which tailors staffing to the intensity of care needed by patients rather than staffing for the total number of patients alone.
- Non-profit communities report a lower incidence of medical problems such as bed-sores.
- Non-profit communities are often more able to respond to the needs of those with limited incomes who need care.[5]

In the interest of full disclosure, Presbyterian Senior Living is one of the largest nonprofit providers of senior care in the country. However, the information shared in its publication is in line with

---

4. Zamora, "Life and Death in Assisted Living."
5. Presbyterian Senior Living, *Clearing up Differences*, 4–5.

information available from other organizations, such as the Center for Medicare Advocacy.

From my own experience I wish I could make an unqualified recommendation, for-profit or nonprofit, one way or another, but I can't. Years ago, while visiting a nonprofit skilled nursing home that my denomination had a hand in establishing, I encountered a situation that I dutifully reported to an administrator. I was told it was none of my business and nothing could be done about it. When I told the chairman of the board about it, he just raised his hands and shrugged his shoulders. In my book, all facilities have pluses and minuses, and all of them need scrutiny.

Quality of Life

Once I visited a church member suffering from Alzheimer's disease who had fallen down a flight of stairs and had multiple fractures in one of her arms. She was operated on, and survived, but I was shocked when I saw her as she came out of recovery. Her arm was fixed in place by a series of metal rods that protruded from layers of bandages, making her look a little like a figure from *Star Wars*. My first thought was that no one told the surgeon she had advanced Alzheimer's! She would not understand what had happened to her, would not remember what the rods were for, and would not be able to keep from hitting them against who knows what when walking around. It proved to be disastrous for her. One complication followed another until she finally died without ever regaining the use of her arm.

In the same way that dementia sufferers are causing surgeons to reconsider how things are done, housing for dementia is especially trying. There are so many issues, so many things that go awry. Yet it is important to remember that a diagnosis of dementia does not end the patient's personhood. No matter what the cause of dementia, no matter how far advanced it may be, your loved one is still a child of God and needs the care and attention he or she deserves. Whether at-home care is provided, or a form of residential care, or a memory care facility is used, whether for-profit or nonprofit, quality of life is always a matter to consider. We will not "warehouse" our elderly.

The Alzheimer's Association's *Campaign for Quality Residential Care* lists the "fundamentals" of dementia care:

- People with dementia are able to experience joy, comfort, meaning and growth in their lives.
- Optimal care occurs within a social environment that supports the development of healthy relationships between staff, family and residents.
- Good dementia care involves assessment of a resident's abilities; care planning and provision; strategies for addressing behavioral and communication changes; appropriate staffing patterns; and an assisted living or nursing home environment that fosters community.
- Each person with dementia is unique, having a different constellation of abilities and need for support, which change over time as the disease progresses.
- Good dementia care involves using information about a resident to develop "person-centered" strategies, which are designed to ensure that services are tailored to each individual's circumstances.[6]

Quality of Life and Intimacy

One of the most heartbreaking scenes I have ever witnessed involved a man visiting his wife in a memory care unit and being introduced by his wife to her new "boyfriend." She did not know her husband, but she sure knew her friend. They giggled together, held hands, and shared whispered conversational asides. On the way out the door, the husband told me, "I'm not sure what I'm supposed to think about that."

Dementia changes every aspect of a person's life, including sexuality. For some people intimate relationships become less important, for others they become more so. Inhibitions are often

---

6. *Dementia Care Practice*, 5.

dropped. Language may become much more direct and coarse. Issues of consent become muddled.

In addition to all of the information to consider about residential care given in the section above, you will want to know if the home has policies on privacy and sexuality. Ask what happens if a resident shows affection or sexual feelings towards another resident or a staff member. And what about same-sex relationships? Will they be treated with as much respect as heterosexual relationships? Remember, a person's civil rights are not suspended because of dementia.

De Hogeweyk in Amsterdam

I recently saw a television feature about a wonderfully creative nursing home in Amsterdam that takes seriously the "fundamentals" listed above. It is called De Hogeweyk[7] and its basic idea is "all-day reminiscence therapy" with the result that residents are more active and require less medication than in traditional settings.

The Hogeweyk complex is set out like a village with a town square, supermarket, hairdressing salon, theatre, pub, and café-restaurant—as well as twenty-three "houses." Each house reflects a style that is familiar for the six or seven people who live in that house.

Doctors, nurses, and other caregivers aim to make the experience of living there as normal as possible for the residents. They shop at the supermarket and assist with preparing and cooking as they would at home. Caregivers wear normal daytime clothing rather than clinical clothing and fit into a role that the dementia sufferers are likely to be comfortable with. Residents in each house have their own large bedroom and meet with other residents to share the living room, kitchen and dining room. There are no locks on the doors, and residents are free to walk or cycle around the village.

To maintain the "fake reality" that those living at Hogeweyk are comfortable with, the staff are instructed not to correct the residents as they talk about memories, background, and history.

---

7. http://hogeweyk.dementiavillage.com.

At the same time, the staff will not deceive the patients if directly asked, truthfully stating that the residents are in a place where they can receive care for their condition. (Because of the nature of dementia, the residents can remember the distant past but not the present, so even truthful answers given by the staff will be forgotten quickly.)

What a marvelous way to handle dementia! (Does it remind you of Main Street, USA, in Walt Disney World? Maybe "the mouse" isn't just for kids.) Other organizations are slowly catching on. For instance, there are now 260 Green House Homes in thirty-two states "dedicated to reimagining the traditional nursing home." Hopefully, if you need it, there will be one near you—or one like it.

Conclusion

The bottom line for me is that the type of facility I want for my mother (should that time come), or for myself or my wife, is one that looks and feels less like a hospital and more like a real home. It doesn't have to be a high-class hotel, but it doesn't need to feel "institutional" either.

It may take more than one attempt to find a place that fits, but keep trying! Caring for someone with dementia may be much more intense than caring for a person with other health issues, but it can be done. In fact, it must be done. And there are plenty of places and people and resources that can help. At the conclusion of this book I have listed print and online resources that may prove helpful.

In spite of all of the above, the most common theme I hear from families about deciding on how to care for a member of their family, even if that decision is to keep them at home, is guilt. Terrible, heart-rending, gut-twisting guilt.

8

Guilt

> When they call the roll in the Senate, the Senators do not know whether to answer "Present" or "Not guilty."
> —TEDDY ROOSEVELT

DAMNED IF YOU DO, damned if you don't: the nearly universal feeling a child, spouse, or guardian has over the decision to put a loved one in an assisted living facility or a nursing home. My own mother has told us (my sisters and I) for years, "Don't you dare put me away some place." Only recently have I begun to caution her not to say that on the grounds that we never know what we might face coming down the pike. She agrees, but still says she doesn't want to be put in "some home!"

Caregiver Guilt

Caregiver guilt can be an ocean of despair. Carol Bradley Bursack, who writes for several caregiving websites, says: "If there's one emotion that nearly anyone caring for vulnerable people can count on it is guilt. We feel guilty about a decision to take some kind of action. We feel guilty about a decision to wait. We feel guilty about asking others to help. We feel guilty about not asking for help."[1]

Presbyterian Senior Living itemizes "trigger" events that cause guilt, such as:

- Having an enjoyable experience without your loved one
- Feelings of relief without them
- Making a medical decision for them, like a DNR order
- Becoming dissatisfied with the care or lack of attention from the home
- Feeling the need to always be by their side[2]

This list is endless. If there's one thing Americans know how to do, it's feel guilt. Caregiver guilt is related to survivor guilt, which occurs when a person lives through a traumatic event that others do not survive. People who believe it is unfair that they survived when others died, or believe they did not do enough to save the lives of others, are experiencing such guilt. These two feelings, of unfairness and of not doing enough, are rampant among dementia patient caregivers.

In 1970 almost all of the members of the Marshall University football team were on a plane that crashed just short of the runway, killing everyone on board. The movie about it, *We Are Marshall*, follows a coach who gave his seat on the plane to another coach, a player who was injured and did not make the trip, and another player who overslept and missed the flight. All are haunted by feelings of guilt that affect them long after the crash.

I lived near Huntington, West Virginia, in 1984 when Marshall's football team had its first winning season after the crash. I can't tell you how cathartic that season was. It was as though the team's victories removed layers of guilt and depression that had been smothering the whole region. That's another thing that guilt does: it dampens and lessens everything we do.

---

1. Bursack, "Unearned Guilt."
2. Juliano, "Coping with Guilt."

Guilt

Remote Caregivers' Guilt

If guilt over trying to care for a loved one with dementia isn't bad enough, the distance that many of us have to deal with amplifies the problem. Once upon a time, families lived close by. Now, about 15 percent of all caregivers live more than one hour away from the one being cared for. How can guilt NOT be a factor? Am I visiting enough? Am I calling enough? Am I doing enough? On the other hand, how can I? I have a life of my own, with demands of its own, with constraints I cannot eliminate.

My wife and I are part of a neighborhood "walking group." Nearly every morning one of us is making plans to visit mom or dad, or to take one of them to the doctor, or is somehow fretting over how to address this or that concern.

Isabella Yosuico wrote an excellent article, "Tips for Long Distance Caregivers," that acknowledges, "First, there's the stress of juggling caregiving logistics. Then there's the communication challenges. And then there's the guilt for just not being able to live closer."[3] It goes on to give valuable advice for staying connected with the on-site caregivers, neighbors, and health care staff, as well as suggesting strategies for managing all that needs to be done.

A family in our congregation dealt very practically with remote care. One sibling lived in town close to their mother. The other sibling lived several hours away. So, the two of them divided up "who would do what." The one in town took on weekly visits, doctor's appointments, that sort of thing. The one out of town took on the finances. An unexpected benefit of this arrangement, I was told, was that the one in town was able to be the "nice guy" while the one out of town was able to "play hardball" when necessary.

Guilt, Guilt, and More Guilt

Like other emotions, there is no single explanation for guilt. But like most troublesome states of mind, we grab on to anything that can help us deal with it.

3. Yosuico, "Tips for Long Distance."

Do Not Cast Me Away

An article written by Susan Krauss Whitbourne for *Psychology Today* lists five types of guilt that come our way: 1) Guilt for something you did; 2) Guilt for something that you did not do, but wanted to; 3) Guilt for something that you think you did; 4) Guilt that you did not do enough to help someone; and 5) Guilt that you are doing better than someone else.[4]

I read this list to a group of people, each of whom had caregiving responsibilities for a person with dementia. I asked them to raise their hands as I went through the list to indicate if they had experienced that type of guilt. All of them raised their hands on all five types!

The first one, guilt for something you did, is supposed to mean guilt for something you did wrong. Causing harm. Lying. Cheating. Stealing. That sort of thing. Finding appropriate residential care for a person who can no longer safely stay at home is not doing something wrong. Signing a DNR order for a parent with severe dementia is not wrong. But it can still feel emotionally wrong!

Guilt for something that you did not do "but wanted to" refers to thinking about violating our moral code or planning to break the law. However, some caregivers—pushed to the ends of their endurance—inevitably wonder (fleetingly) what it would be like to no longer bear the burden of caring for someone. One woman I know laughingly told me about finding her father outside the house one winter evening and thinking about not going out to get him. She referred to him as her own personal "Houdini."

Feeling guilty about something we think we did is a tough one. We are able to rationalize our way out of things and into things. If we think mom was miserable in "that home"—and we put her there—we may be miserable ourselves, no matter how irrational a thought that might be. (I mean, she was miserable at home, so why wouldn't she be miserable elsewhere?)

Guilt that you did not do enough to help someone might be the great "tie that binds" all dementia patient caregivers together. The fact is, there is no limit to what can be done in helping a loved one with dementia. Our obligation to them ends only at their

---

4. Whitbourne, "Definitive Guide to Guilt."

death (or ours), and if we have been left in charge of an estate, it can go on for years afterwards.

Finally, guilt that you are doing better than someone else may be the cruelest way we torture ourselves. After all we have done, all that we have endured, the sacrifices we've made, the costs we've paid—financially, emotionally, physically—when our loved one is gone we are robbed of the peace of mind of knowing that we did our best because of this residual guilt.

Tom Hanks's character in the movie *A League of Their Own* chastised a player who was overcome by the difficulty she faced by saying, "There's no crying in baseball." Likewise, there is no rest for the weary caregiver consumed by guilt. Once we are in the game—whether we choose to be or not—we cannot stop playing.

Growing Up

Caring for a loved one with dementia may just become a terrible sort of rite of passage. It may mean we caregivers are now "adults" in our own right. I have heard it said that we as individuals do not become fully grown up until the parent we are closest to has died, that we are truly on our own once that happens. With dementia, death occurs slowly. We care for mom or dad, we work to keep them as healthy as possible for as long as possible, and one day we realize they are no longer who they once were. This means we are no longer who we thought we were, too!

The irony in all of this is that as children we spend our entire lives working toward a peer relationship with our parents only to have it dissolve on their end, not ours. It takes a great deal of psychic energy to get there, on our part, and on the part of our parents, who sometimes aren't aware how difficult it is for us to join them on their playing field. How sad when we realize our efforts to join in their world will not last long due to disease!

But still we do it and we are grateful for whatever time we have with them.

Role-Reversal

If I had a dollar for every time I heard someone say something like, "He's the child now and I'm the parent," I'd be a wealthy man. Be careful here; these are murky waters.

> While relationships between parents and children clearly change over time, there is no such thing as a "reversal." For one thing, unless specific powers of attorney, etc. are granted, we do not actually have any legal responsibility for our parents in the same way that parents have legal obligations to children. Adult children have no automatic authority over aging parents. Aging parents, unless deemed mentally incapacitated, have all the legal rights and responsibilities as anyone else—quite unlike children.[5]

Positive Guilt

Not all guilt is a bad thing. Sometimes it can prompt us to actions we would rather not take. In one of Garrison Keillor's monologues about Lake Woebegone, one of his characters has been trying to quit smoking but is rummaging around the bathroom in the middle of the night looking for a cigarette that might be hidden somewhere. The noise he makes wakes up his young daughter who comes to see what is going on. In his nicotine-withdrawal panic, he doesn't see the girl come into the room and runs into her, knocking her against a wall. Her injuries are minor, but the guilt he feels at hurting her over his need for a smoke drives him to quit cigarettes once and for all.

Guilt over what to do for our demented loved one may, in fact, be a positive thing. It may stem from a recognition that he or she is still a human being, created in the image of God. Guilt over their condition may prevent us from "warehousing" the elderly. It may grow out of our fear that someday we will hear the word

---

5. "Role Reversal with an Aging Parent," https://www.sageminder.com/Caregiving/Relationships/RoleReversal.aspx.

Guilt

"Alzheimer's" applied to us. But even so, if such feelings remind us that those with dementia are human—not used to be human or once were human, but are human—then questions about the utility of providing care for them, or the social costs thereof, will be more compassionately answered.

Conclusion

The nearly universal prescription for guilt over caregiving is to talk about it. You can't give it away by talking about it (there are emotional adjustments that have to be made), but it's a start. But it does make a difference who you talk to. Your local Alzheimer's Association should have a list of support groups. There are dozens of online groups.

65 million Americans care for a chronically ill family member, yet each one tends to care "alone." It need not be that way! Guilt, if not creatively handled, can make a bad situation much worse. There are professionals who can help. Clergy, yes. But also geriatric social workers and elder law attorneys. Both are trained to help you through the morass of issues facing every dementia patient caregiver. According to eCaring.com,

> Aging-savvy social workers serve as "navigators" through the complicated healthcare and social service systems. They help families by gathering information about the array of services available to them, coordinating care across various health systems, facilitating family support, and providing direct counseling services.[6]

Elder law attorneys, also known as elder care attorneys,

> are advocates for the elderly and their loved ones. Most elder law attorneys handle a wide range of legal matters affecting an older or disabled person, including issues related to health care, long term care planning,

---

6. "What Does a Geriatric Social Worker Do?" https://ecaring.com/what-does-a-geriatric-social-worker-do/.

guardianship, retirement, Social Security, Medicare/Medicaid, and other important matters.[7]

A consultation with someone who has dealt with dementia patients on this level can go a long way toward alleviating at least some of the guilt you might feel.

---

7. "What Does an Elder Law Attorney Do?" https://elder.findlaw.com/what-is-elder-law/what-does-an-elder-law-attorney-do-.html.

9

Paying for Care

As a child, my aunt Olive had a friend who was invisible to others. Topsy lived at the back of the garden. That this was just her imagination Olive always strenuously denied. And when she developed dementia many years later Topsy again faithfully kept her company.

—A.J. BEIRENS

ONE OF THE STORIES making the rounds in our neighborhood is of a couple who moved from Chattanooga to a retirement community in Florida. The husband died and the wife developed dementia. She is now living in a state-supported facility, having gone through a small fortune. The people who tell me about her shudder at the thought of not having enough money to be well taken care of should a catastrophic illness or dementia befall them.

I don't blame them. The difference in the quality of care from facility to facility can be enormous. And heaven help those who have no one to watch out for them! How does one pay for dementia care, anyway? A news feature on NPR's *Morning Edition* in 2016 began this way: "First, Alzheimer's takes a person's memory. Then it takes their family's money."[1]

The first hint I received at just how expensive a long-term illness could be was while I was pastor of a congregation in West Virginia in the 1990s. The husband of a couple I knew became ill with a vague diagnosis (he just "wasn't right anymore") which I now suspect was some type of dementia. He was elderly as was his wife, but she decided to keep him at home with around the clock nursing help. She eventually paid for three "shifts" a day, seven days a week, for more than three years, at $20 an hour. Do the math!

According to the Alzheimer's Association, Alzheimer's disease is the most expensive medical condition in the United States. It cost Americans an estimated $214 billion in 2014. Estimates are that it cost $277 billion in 2018, a number projected to increase to as much as $1.1 trillion by 2050. According to a 2015 study, the average cost of dementia care (over a five-year period) was $287,038, compared to $175,136 (heart disease) and $173,383 (cancer).[2] It hardly needs to be stated that it behooves every family to put thought into how they can deal with the financial implications of this disease should it prove necessary.

The Alzheimer's Association lists six primary ways families pay for dementia care: insurance, employee benefits, retirement benefits, personal savings, investments and property, government assistance, and community support services. Do not forget that geriatric social workers and elder care attorneys can help you wade through these options.

Insurance

For most people over the age of sixty-five, insurance means Medicare. Established in 1966, Medicare is a national health insurance plan providing for Americans who have worked and paid into the system through the payroll tax. It also provides health insurance

1. Hamilton, "Big Financial Costs."
2. "Facts and Figures," https://www.alz.org/alzheimers-dementia/facts-figures.

to younger people with disability status determined by the Social Security Administration, as well as people with end-stage renal disease and amyotrophic lateral sclerosis. About fifty-five million people are currently covered by Medicare. But the term "covered" is misleading. On average, Medicare pays for approximately half of the health care expenses of those enrolled in it. Surprised? Among other things, Medicare does not pay for hearing aids, dental work, eye exams, podiatry, and nursing-home care. But it does cover short-term rehab stays at a nursing home after a hospitalization and can pay for rehab and in-home therapy for a limited period of time.

Insurance Supplements

The AARP has a wealth of helpful information on Medicare supplement insurance plans. These plans are from private insurers and are designed to complement your Medicare coverage by helping with some of the out-of-pocket expenses not paid by Medicare. Such policies are standardized by law and one company's "Plan F" will have the same provisions as "Plan F" by another company. However, none of the so-called "Medigap" policies cover long-term care to help you bathe, dress, eat, or use the bathroom. Nor do any of them cover private-duty nursing.

Long-Term Care Insurance

Several decades ago, long-term care insurance was introduced as a way to provide the nursing home coverage lacking in Medicare. But the industry is now in turmoil as things simply did not work out as expected. An article entitled "Why Long-Term Care Insurance Is Becoming a Tougher Call" explains:

> When the first long-term care policies came on the market in the mid-1970s, insurers based their projections for premium costs and payouts on life insurance data. They told consumers that premiums would rise minimally, if at all, over the life of their policy.

But people lived longer and health care costs grew faster than the insurers ever expected. Seniors who bought low-priced policies in the 1980s and 1990s lived for years with chronic and expensive-to-manage conditions like Alzheimer's disease or Parkinson's disease. Worst of all, low interest rates meant that insurers earned very little on the premiums they collected—money they'd need to pay future claims.[3]

There are now "hybrid" policies that combine life insurance with long-term care benefits, but the best way to plan for future needs still seems to be an old-fashioned one: save for it, if you can.

Employee Benefits & Retirement Benefits

The only employee benefits due to a person still working, even though he or she might be in the early stages of dementia, might be something like sick leave or short-term disability. The primary retirement benefits are whatever funds have accrued in an IRA or employee-funded retirement plan. A person under fifty-nine and a half years old diagnosed with dementia can withdraw funds without an early withdrawal penalty.

Personal Savings, Investments, and Property

The Alzheimer's Association does not try to sugar coat this. It says, "Personal assets—belonging to the person with dementia or other family members—can be sources of income to help pay for care."[4] Make sure to re-read this: "Personal assets—belonging to the person with dementia or other family members—can be sources of income to help pay for care." Everything is up for grabs: stocks, bonds, savings accounts, real estate, even jewelry or artwork.

Without trying to be alarmist, it seems to me that one of the things our rising cost of health care has brought about is a

3. Ostrov, "Long-Term Insurance."
4. "Paying for Care," https://www.alz.org/help-support/caregiving/financial-legal-planning/paying-for-care.

transition away from parents working and saving so they can pass on an inheritance to their children to them working and saving to pay for their own catastrophic illness or long-term care.

That being said, personal sources of funding for dementia care might include equity in a home, artwork or jewelry that could be liquidated, real estate, or funds invested in stocks or an IRA. This also might include "family" money, funds contributed by family members who pitch in to keep mom or dad in a certain facility, or who pay for a "sitter" during the day, or for some other need.

An Alzheimer's Association report issued in 2016 found that "friends and family spent, on average, more than $5000 a year of their own money on the expenses of their loved one with dementia, ranging from food to adult diapers."[5] In addition, "more than one-third of these contributors to care who had jobs had to reduce their hours or quit," and "nearly half of the care contributors surveyed had to dip into their savings or retirement funds."[6]

One time I was called upon to meet an attorney at a woman's bedside to witness him taking her last valuable, a large diamond ring, to be sold to help pay for her care. I was told this had to be done as the rest of her estate had already been spent. My only solace in this was knowing that she herself probably did not know the ring was gone.

Government Assistance

A person with dementia may qualify for a number of public programs that provide income support or long-term care services to people who are eligible. This includes Social Security Disability Income (SSDI) for workers younger than sixty-five, Supplemental Security Income (SSI), and Medicaid. And there are some tax deductions and credits that may help offset expenses.[7] The Centers for Medicare and Medical Services website provides information

---

5. Marcus, "Some People Make 'Startling' Sacrifices."

6. Marcus, "Some People Make 'Startling' Sacrifices."

7. "Tax Deductions and Credits," https://www.alz.org/help-support/caregiving/financial-legal-planning/tax-deductions-credits.

on health insurance for the millions of Americans receiving Medicare and/or Medicaid.

Veteran's Benefits

A form of government assistance not mentioned above may be veteran's benefits. There is a VA program called Community Residential Care, which provides "group" care in approximately 1,300 facilities nationwide. Also, the surviving spouse of a veteran is eligible for these benefits as well.

Community Support Services

There are community organizations that provide low-cost services, such as respite care, support groups, transportation, and home-delivered meals. The federal government funds the Administration on Aging. Every state has a Council on Aging. There are numerous Alzheimer's Association offices. The AARP is a great resource. And Christian denominations and their congregations are increasingly offering programs to help families, especially when the patient is "early-stage" and still mobile. More about this will be said in the next chapter.

Medicaid

Probably the most widely used government assistance program that can help with dementia care is Medicaid, but it has requirements that need to be met.

According to the Kaiser Family Foundation, Medicaid prohibits individuals from transferring savings to others in an attempt to qualify for nursing home care without exhausting their assets. Sixty percent of nursing home residents are not on Medicaid at the time of their admittance into a facility. With the average annual cost of nursing home care being $60,000, the longer an individual remains in a facility, the more likely they are to deplete their financial resources and qualify for Medicaid coverage. Even after individuals deplete their assets, they are still required to apply their income, including Social Security and pension checks, towards their care costs, except for an average monthly $30 personal needs allowance.[8]

Many of the websites dealing with Medicaid have a section that addresses "myths" about it. This one, for instance, is "Hardworking middle-class people who save for their retirement years will not need to rely on Medicaid for long-term care." The reply is: "Medicare and private health insurance do not cover most long-term care (LTC) expenses, making Medicaid the "safety net" for many middle-income persons. [However] to receive Medicaid LTC services, these individuals must become impoverished and deplete almost all of their assets."[9]

Here's another myth pertinent to dementia care: "Family caregivers don't care for their own anymore, and simply rely on Medicaid." The reply, "More than 90 percent of persons age 65 and older with disabilities who receive help with daily activities are helped by unpaid informal caregivers; 66 percent receive no paid care at all, relying entirely on informal caregivers. The estimated economic value of informal caregivers' contributions in 2006 ($350 billion) exceeded total Medicaid spending for both health care and LTC ($299 billion in 2006)."[10]

The reality of dementia care is that for most families it is paid for out of a patch-worked combination of sources.

---

8. "Most and Least Expensive States for Long-Term Care (2017)," https://www.medicaidannuity.com/states-cost-of-long-term-care/.

9. "Myths about the Medicaid Program," https://www.aarp.org/health/medicare-insurance/info-11-2008/fs146_myths.html.

10. "Myths about the Medicaid Program," https://www.aarp.org/health/medicare-insurance/info-11-2008/fs146_myths.html.

How Do Families Manage?

Remember the woman who watched the televised tribute to Pat Summitt and then remarked, "No one made a fuss over me when I lost my mind"? According to her daughter,

> Mom's care was really based around her physical issues more than her dementia. This was a full-time job for (the family) for 7 1/2 years. Remember that she had Crohn's disease and had to have a couple of major surgeries before we even suspected the mental decline. But, we think her mental decline was more rapid with the multitude of surgeries/anesthesia effects.[11]

Her mother was a moving target for much of this time, shuttling back and forth between her own home and the daughter's home. At times she required nursing care, at other times an untrained sitter/companion worked well. Fortunately, a long-term health care policy included private duty coverage.

This family went through the gauntlet of available help, including a comprehensive driving course, a geriatric assessment program, and an elder care attorney. Their goal was to keep mom in her own home as long as possible. Eventually, she was moved into an assisted living facility, but still needed additional help. Her last few months were spent in a skilled nursing facility.

In retrospect, her daughter says,

> What we might have done differently was to leave her in her house and skip Assisted Living, but that would not have afforded us the ability to clean her house out and get it sold before her death. It would have been so hard emotionally, to have done that after her death. I feel like I could have moved her in with me if I had had just one of her major health issues to deal with, but not both dementia and the physical problems. She trained us for many years to care for the elderly and make those tough

---

11. Personal communication with the author.

calls (she was a nurse), so I think she will one day tell us we did the right thing.[12]

Conclusion

Every patient is different, every family handles dementia care in their own unique way, and every financial consideration is answered accordingly. It seems better, though, if there are more people involved than fewer. One way or another, families "cobble together" what needs to be done to pay for dementia care. Surely, though, a little planning ahead could help in the long run.

---

12. Personal communication with the author.

10

Finding Support

> People think it's a terrible tragedy when somebody has Alzheimer's. But in my mother's case, it's different. My mother has been unhappy all her life. For the first time in her life, she's happy.
>
> —AMY TAN

WHILE VISITING WITH A woman whose husband had died with frontotemporal dementia, I asked if she ever thought of using the "adult day care" offered by a local Methodist Church. Her reply struck me to the quick: "Oh, no," she said, "he would have wanted to go to his own church, not another one." He could have been dropped off at *our* church and sat in *my* office with me a few hours each week! We blew a chance to provide support to her and her husband in a time of increasing need. We just didn't think about it. But some congregations are thinking about it, and doing something about it, too.

Finding Support

Adult Day Care

Chattanooga has several facilities for adult day care. Although none are housed in a church, one is run by the Alexian Brothers, a Roman Catholic religious community associated with the rule of St. Augustine. Assisted living communities are sometimes able to offer this service, as are skilled nursing facilities, home care agencies, and medical centers. No matter where they are located, all adult day cares have the same mission: to provide care and companionship for older adults who need assistance during the day, and whose caregivers need respite.

An article on the National Caregivers Library website entitled "What Is Adult Day Care?" lists the following benefits a recipient receives from adult day care:

- It allows him or her to stay in his or her community while the caregiver goes to work
- It gives him or her a break from the caregiver
- It provides needed social interaction
- It provides greater structure to his or her daily activities[1]

According to a publication of the Polis Center, "Adult day care began in Russia in the 1920s and '30s, proliferated in England at mid-century, and moved to the United States in the 1970s, where it grew rapidly."[2] Unfortunately, the same article notes, "Religious organizations have never been a major factor in adult day care."[3] But that seems to be changing.

For example, Prime Time Adult Care, Inc. is a nonprofit organization that originated in 1985 as an outreach ministry of the United Methodist church in Bethel Park, Pennsylvania. It

1. "What is Adult Day Care?" http://www.caregiverslibrary.org/caregivers-resources/grp-caring-for-yourself/hsgrp-support-systems/what-is-adult-day-care-article.aspx.

2. "Congregations and Adult Day Care," https://www.polis.iupui.edu/RUC/Newsletters/Responsive/vol1no1.htm.

3. "Congregations and Adult Day Care," https://www.polis.iupui.edu/RUC/Newsletters/Responsive/vol1no1.htm.

has grown into a five-day-a-week program that is licensed by the Pennsylvania Department of Aging. The goal of Prime Time is "to activate, reinstitute, or maintain function of the elderly clients to the greatest extent of their ability and add to their quality of life."[4]

An older organization dedicated to senior care is based in Louisville, Kentucky. Founded in 1884, Christian Care Communities (a ministry of the Disciples of Christ) "is the largest, faith-based, not-for-profit provider of affordable senior retirement living and long-term care for older adults in Kentucky, serving the physical and emotional needs of older adults."[5] CCC operates adult day care centers in four different Kentucky cities.

While they may not be on every corner, adult day care centers do exist in increasing numbers. Sometimes they are hiding in plain view. Last summer my wife and I were invited to attend a fundraiser for a local organization called "Signal Centers" that began as a program to serve children with cerebral palsy. We learned about its work with children, and then were pleased to hear about its adult services, which include a weekly adult day program, designed to give caregivers respite and offer socialization and activities for senior adults.

Sing from Memory

Your congregation may not be able to pull off an adult day care center (our congregation thought about it, but finally decided against it), but there are other ways you can help meet the needs of aging adults. For instance, if your church has members who love to sing, plus a few who can play an instrument, you could establish a program of "Sing from Memory."

Begun here in Chattanooga by Wayne Evans, who was inspired by a BBC television documentary, Sing from Memory is a ninety minute (or so) program in which everyone sings along to the golden oldies and hymns of their childhood—providing

4. "Adult Daycare," https://www.christumc.net/content.cfm?id=148&ministry_id=1.

5. "Quick Facts," https://www.christiancarecommunities.org/quick-facts/.

Finding Support

needed socialization for both the patient and caregiver. Along with stimulating the Alzheimer's patients' memory, the songfests offer caregivers a way to network with others who are coping with the same problems.

The concept is based on Alzheimer's Association research that has shown the parts of the brain that remember words and tunes are among the last to be affected by the disease. People also associate music with important events and emotions, a connection so strong that just hearing a familiar tune long after the occurrence can still evoke that memory. Wayne says he has been told that some of the "guests" continue to sing or hum tunes they have heard at Sing from Memory for the rest of the day.

A typical Sing from Memory session begins with guests and caregivers gathering at the appointed time (ours is after lunch: persons with dementia often have a hard time with early gatherings). It takes about a half an hour for everyone to get in, get comfortable, mingle, and greet one another. We have simple snacks available and round tables for seating. Because we project lyrics onto a screen at one end of the room, we encourage a "half-moon" seating arrangement. We sometimes have coloring books and colored pencils or crayons on the tables, and bubble wrapping for arthritic fingers to pop.

The first song is always the opening lines of "Hello, Dolly" modified for each person present. Instead of "Hello Dolly, this is Miss Dolly," we sing "Hello Jimmy, this is Mr. Jimmy," or "Hello Helen," or "Hello Mary." Every guest is recognized and sung to.

Then we launch into a series of fifteen to seventeen songs led by our music/video team, with a break in the middle (to give the musicians a rest) with various sorts of activities, trivia, and jokes. Hundreds of songs with lyrics on the screen can be downloaded for free from YouTube, so there is virtually no end of the programmatic "themes" that can be developed. We've featured "working songs" (for Labor Day), cowboy music (Gene Autry, Roy Rogers, etc.), the '50s and '60s (Elvis is big favorite), and old-fashioned gospel hymns. Believe me, if we can do it, your church can, too.

Do Not Cast Me Away

Support Groups

I was recently shown a cartoon. A sign read "Forgetful Folks Support Group." At a podium a newcomer to the group introduces himself, "My name's Bill and I'm forgetful." The members seated in front of him reply in unison, "Hi, Carl!"[6]

One of the benefits of Sing from Memory is that it functions for some of the caregivers as a sort of a support group. Support groups related to those suffering from dementia come in all sorts of configurations. They can be for caregivers only, for persons with dementia only, or may be a mixed group of caregivers and patients. They can be run by "peers" or by professionally trained facilitators. There are support groups that are dementia-specific, such as for Lewy body dementia only, or one that might be restricted to vascular dementia. And online support groups of all kinds are gaining in popularity, such as the ones found on Facebook or run by AARP.

Local Alzheimer's Associations, hospitals, and some memory care facilities encourage and promote support groups (including online ones), and churches are great locations for them, provided they are handicapped accessible. Establish a program like Sing from Memory, add in a support group or two, and you are on your way to becoming a dementia friendly congregation.

Dementia Friendly Congregations

The Discipleship Ministries of the United Methodist Church challenges its congregations to be "dementia friendly." In addition to reminding congregations to take a careful look at their buildings (is the hot water too warm? Are there grab bars in the bathrooms? Are there trip hazards in the hallways?) it suggests "A Dozen Quick Ideas to Become a More Dementia-Friendly Church."

1. Host Alzheimer's and dementia caregiver's support group meetings . . .

---

6. *Speedbump*, Apr 13, 2016. Quoted with permission from the artist, Dave Coverly.

2. Offer a monthly respite time or day for caregivers of members with dementia. Include activities for those who have dementia besides sitting, sleeping, or watching television.

3. Help people with dementia and caregivers look good by sponsoring a quarterly makeover day with area volunteers and cosmetologists.

4. Offer a weekly or monthly special worship service for members with dementia, or designate special Dementia Sundays where the main worship service is designed specifically for those with dementia. Include familiar hymns rather than new ones in the service.

5. Look for talents and abilities in people with dementia that they can develop and share with other people in the church. Affirm them in performing their service by acknowledging and thanking them before the entire church.

6. Train church leaders and members in dementia awareness and strategies for dealing with potential challenges that might arise.

7. Offer a Memory Café where the memory-impaired and their caregivers can gather to remember. Consider a workshop on making memory boxes for members with dementia and their caregivers.

8. Have leaders of the church agree to and sign a code of behavior for interacting with members with dementia. (Examples of this would be listening patiently when members with dementia tell the same story over and over again; listening to what people with dementia are saying; avoiding correcting people with dementia when they do something improperly.)

9. Offer a resource or reading center on dementia as well as a dementia newsletter with a review of some of the latest news on Alzheimer's.

10. Develop a visitation team to visit members with dementia when they become homebound or move to a skilled medical center. Include regular Communion delivery and videos of worship services in the visits.

11. Research, develop, and print a community resource guide for caregivers of those who have dementia.

12. Develop a daily or weekly prayer chain and checking-in program for the families and caregivers of those who have dementia to minister to their mental, emotional, and spiritual well-being.[7]

Other denominations have similar resources to share, as well. For instance, the United Church of Christ promotes a "Mental Health Toolkit" that covers a wide spectrum of issues beyond dementia.[8] And the Presbyterian Church (USA) offers a downloadable study entitled *Caring for People with Alzheimer's*.[9]

Virtual Dementia Tour

There are now websites with programs devoted to what are being called "Virtual Dementia Tours." The first one I read about was developed by geriatric specialist P. K. Beville, founder of Second Wind Dreams, which markets reasonably priced VDT kits "to help sensitize caregivers in the area of dementia care." This is an easy way to introduce teens and young adults to the realities of dementia, not to mention aiding caregivers in understanding what their loved ones may be experiencing.

According to NextAvenue.org, a Virtual Dementia Tour "employs four components to alter the subject's senses and perception and simulate the day-to-day experiences of people with dementia and Alzheimer's." 1. Goggles that simulate "macular degeneration, diminished depth perception and loss of peripheral vision." 2. Shoe inserts "that simulate uncomfortable pins-and-needles sensations in the bottom of the feet." 3. Gloves "that hinder the wearer's sense

---

7. "The Dementia-Friendly Church," https://www.umcdiscipleship.org/resources/the-dementia-friendly-church.

8. "Dementia/Alzheimer's Congregational Toolkit," http://mhn-ucc.blogspot.com/p/ucc-mental-health-network.html.

9. *Caring for People with Alzheimer's*, https://www.pcusastore.com/Products/PL0093/caring-for-people-with-alzheimers.aspx?bCategory=PCSTU!PC.

of touch and impair the ability to feel through his or her fingers." And, 4. Headphones equipped with a "confusion tape" playing in the background.[10]

An article on Alzheimer's Reading Room by Bob DeMarco says that he tried it and "it works." DeMarco wrote: "While doing the Virtual Dementia Tour you become completely disoriented and disconcerted. Your brain just won't do what you want it to do. Imagine that."[11]

Other Options

The ways to be intentionally involved in helping care for those with dementia, and with supporting their caregivers, are virtually endless. Be a "mentor" to someone with dementia: schedule time with that person on a regular basis, something the caregiver will be able to depend on. Or be a "pen pal" to someone. Write to them, send them notes and cards to remind them that they are not forgotten. Get involved with your local "meals on wheels." You will be amazed at how many elderly persons live alone and for whom you would be a bright spot in their day. Check to see if there is a Council on Aging in your city. Volunteer through it. And please contact your local Alzheimer's Association for information and support on whatever you and your congregation get involved in.

Conclusion

One of the great gifts we can give to those with dementia is to enjoy being with them. Even though they are enduring mental and physical decline, consider them your teachers; you be the student.

I once led a Bible study at an assisted living facility. We gathered in a circle and worked our way through the gospel of Mark's rendition of Holy Week. When I finished I asked if there were any

---

10. "Take the Virtual Dementia Tour," https://www.nextavenue.org/take-virtual-dementia-tour/.

11. DeMarco, "Virtual Dementia Tour Program."

comments. One woman spoke up about how awful the fire was. At first, I didn't know what she meant—was she referring to a fire in Mark?—until she said she saw it on television. She meant the fire at the Notre Dame Cathedral in Paris, which had just happened! We all laughed because I was the one who was confused!

11

Elder Abuse

> The afternoon knows what the morning never suspected.
> —ROBERT FROST

ONE DAY I VISITED an elderly member of our congregation who had no children and no other relatives, but who had a "family" that looked after her. This is what I found.

After being let inside by a woman I had never met before, I found our member in a hospital bed in the front room. The heat was on high, the drapes were closed, a television was blaring, and there was a stale, musty odor. Formerly, the room had been tastefully decorated with antiques, but it was now almost bare. As was the rest of the house. In fact, her room was the only room on the first floor that appeared to be lived in. She herself was unbathed. We didn't have much of a conversation as she was bedridden due to a stroke, and her speech was impaired. But I was able to have a conversation with the caregiver.

The story was that she and her family had "adopted" our parishioner. After years of housekeeping and generally looking after her, they had been "asked" to take a more active role in her care. This entailed moving out of their home and moving into her home.

They lived upstairs. They took over the checkbook. They drove her car. What happened to the antiques? They had had to sell them in order to pay for her care. And just who was caring for her anyway? The housekeeper, her husband, a grown son, and a daughter-in-law: all living upstairs, all eating there, all being paid for their efforts at caring for our elderly church member out of the checkbook that they themselves commandeered.

It took a few months, but eventually an elder care attorney was able to rescue this sickly woman from those who had moved into her home. Although most of her estate had been plundered, her home was sold and she was able to live out the rest of her days in one of the nursing homes in our area. We visited her often, and the care she received was a 100-percent improvement on what had been happening before.

The Dark Side of Caregiving

The National Institute on Aging (NIA) says:

> Abuse can happen to anyone—no matter the person's age, sex, race, religion, or ethnic or cultural background. Each year, hundreds of thousands of adults over the age of 60 are abused, neglected, or financially exploited. This is called elder abuse.
>
> Abuse can happen in many places, including the older person's home, a family member's house, an assisted living facility, or a nursing home.[1]

Furthermore, elder abuse happens in all sorts of ways: physical, emotional, neglect, abandonment, sexual, financial, and health care fraud. There are probably types of abuse I've left out!

The NIA website warns that "most victims of abuse are women, but some are men. Likely targets are older people who have no family or friends nearby and people with disabilities, memory problems, or dementia." Furthermore, "Abuse can happen to any older person, but often affects those who depend on others for

---

1. "Elder Abuse," https://www.nia.nih.gov/health/elder-abuse.

help with activities of everyday life—including bathing, dressing, and taking medicine."[2]

It is thought that as many as one in ten seniors experience some form of elder abuse every year, which means around five million victims. The sobering reality is that there is more elder abuse than child or spousal abuse combined. Seniors, especially those with dementia, are terribly vulnerable. Unfortunately, most of those abusing our seniors are family members or people they have known and trusted for years.

Financial Abuse

If only I had a dime for every time I heard about someone's mother being taken advantage of by a telemarking scam. The Tennessee Commission on Aging and Disability reports that stealing from the elderly is all too common and all too easy.

> Common acts of fraud involve larceny, embezzlement, forgery, issuing false documents or checks, destruction of wills, breach of fiduciary duty, and the violation of applicable consumer protection statutes.
> Elderly people are typically financially stable. They tend to own their homes, receive pensions, and may have excellent credit and savings in the bank. They are also quite trusting, a trait that can be attributed to their generation and how they were raised. Con artists know this and exploit it for their own gain. All elderly are at risk, but those suffering from a debilitating illness like Alzheimer's disease may be especially vulnerable.[3]

In response to widespread fraud, the AARP proposes a seven-step plan to protect our loved ones:

- When a person is still mentally sharp, help him or her make a plan that designates power of attorney and health care directives ...

2. "Elder Abuse," https://www.nia.nih.gov/health/elder-abuse.

3. "Beware of Fraud," https://www.tn.gov/aging/learn-about/elder-abuse/fraud.html.

- Stay connected with older loved ones through regular phone calls, visits or emails.
- Develop a relationship with your parent's caregiver(s)
- Become a "trusted contact" to monitor bank account and brokerage activity.
- Sign up for a service such as EverSafe [or something similar] to track financial activity and notify an advocate of unusual withdrawals or spending.
- Set up direct deposit for checks so others don't have to cash them.
- Do not sign any documents that you don't understand.[4]

Health Care Fraud

Health care fraud is on the rise, with dementia patients accounting for a significant portion. This is not a caregiver problem. The issue is with medical providers: with nursing homes and hospitals, HMOs and Insurance companies, hospices and home health agencies, and sometimes doctors and nurses.

For instance, in June 2015, federal officials charged 243 people with Medicare fraud involving more than $700 million of fraudulent billing.[5] In July 2016, three Florida residents were charged with an alleged Medicare fraud and money laundering scheme that netted participants $1 billion since 2009. In one case last year the Justice Department charged more than four hundred people across the country in a major crackdown on health care fraud that was costing the federal government $1.3 billion in false Medicare and Medicaid billings.

The most discouraging health care fraud pertaining to people with dementia has to be those cases involving hospice organizations. Evidently, it is fairly easy for hospice management to manipulate their records of how much in-home care a patient receives.

---

4. Rosengren, "7 Ways to Prevent Financial Elder Abuse."
5. Chappell, "Doctors, Nurses among 243 Charged."

Elder Abuse

In some cases, a hospice providing in-home care has been known to pressure a family to move mom or dad to a hospice care facility, after which it can bill Medicare at much higher rates.

No matter who is providing care for your loved one, it is imperative that you know what should be legally provided—and what is actually being dispensed. Every state has specific legislation that covers medical providers. Your local Council on Aging can help with this.

Physical Abuse

The most obvious form of physical abuse is bodily harm caused by hitting or pushing or slapping. But there is more to it than that. Physical abuse may also include "scratching, biting, choking, suffocation, pushing, shoving, shaking, slapping, kicking, stomping, pinching, and burning."[6] Such things as the inappropriate use of drugs, restraints, or confinement are also physical abuse.

According to HelpGuide, warning signs of physical abuse include:

- Unexplained signs of injury, such as bruises, welts, or scars, especially if they appear symmetrically on two sides of the body
- Broken bones, sprains, or dislocations
- Report of drug overdose or apparent failure to take medication regularly (a prescription has more remaining than it should)
- Broken eyeglasses or frames
- Signs of being restrained, such as rope marks on wrists
- Caregiver's refusal to allow you to see the elder alone[7]

---

6. "Elder Abuse: Definitions," https://www.cdc.gov/violenceprevention/elderabuse/definitions.html.

7. "Elder Abuse and Neglect," https://www.helpguide.org/articles/abuse/elder-abuse-and-neglect.htm.

Every state has an Adult Protective Services (APS) agency with a toll-free hotline for reporting suspected abuse. If you encounter what you interpret as abuse, do not confront the abuser(s) yourself, contact APS. In most states, this kind of report can be anonymous.

Emotional Abuse

The Centers for Disease Control describe emotional abuse as:

> verbal or nonverbal behavior that results in the infliction of anguish, mental pain, fear, or distress. Examples include behaviors intended to humiliate (e.g., calling names or insults), threaten (e.g., expressing an intent to initiate nursing home placement), isolate (e.g., seclusion from family or friends), or control (e.g., prohibiting or limiting access to transportation, telephone, money or other resources).[8]

The website of Nursing Home Abuse Center has an even more extensive list:

- Blaming the victim
- Scapegoating the victim
- Engaging in demeaning behavior toward the elder
- Humiliating the victim
- Ridiculing the victim
- Ignoring the needs of the elderly person
- Terrorizing the elderly person
- Behaving menacingly toward the elder
- Intimidating the elder
- Isolating the elder from friends, family or social occasions
- Yelling at the victim

---

8. "Elder Abuse: Definitions," https://www.cdc.gov/violenceprevention/elderabuse/definitions.html.

- Using threatening behavior against the elder[9]

It is thought that emotional abuse is the most common form of abuse against seniors, and those with dementia are the highest risk.

Neglect

Neglect is the failure to provide necessities, including food, clothing, shelter, medical care, or a safe environment. A few years ago one of our members fell in her assisted living apartment. She lay on the floor for several days before she was found. Should she have been checked on by the staff? Daily contact was supposed to be one of the services offered!

I cannot tell you how many times I have visited an elderly person in a nursing home and found them with a "wet" bed or suffering from bed sores or wearing filthy clothes or waiting for assistance to go to the bathroom. On these occasions I have found the nursing station and put in a request for help. One of the ways to cut down on neglect—especially in a facility—is by visiting a patient often, and at different times of day.

Mostly, though, the kind of neglect I see is when the children live away and have not yet come to grips with their loved one's dementia. Mom or dad insist they are doing well, even though that is painfully not true. Children take them at their word as they always have. In these cases, if the church has a relationship with the entire family, children may be convinced that it is time to make some sort of arrangements to see that their parent is taken care of.

It must be pointed out in any conversation about elder abuse that false accusations of such are very common. An elderly person who has dementia may claim to be a victim of abuse when it isn't so. Attorneys who are experts in elder law can give advice if you find yourself under investigation for a false charge of elder abuse.

---

9. "Emotional Abuse," https://www.nursinghomeabusecenter.com/elder-abuse/types/emotional-abuse/.

Abandonment

The website Elder.FindLaw.com defines "elder abandonment" as "the purposeful and permanent desertion of an elderly person. The victim may be left at a hospital, a nursing home, or in a public location."[10] This actually happens! A person gives a phony address and phone number to the hospital admissions staff and cannot be contacted about the care of the person they've admitted. How easy must it be to simply drop a person off at a mall and drive away?[11]

Sexual Abuse

Nursing Home Abuse Center reports that senior or elder sexual abuse includes "any sexual contact with an elder who, because of mental illness or dementia, cannot communicate their disapproval of the behavior against them or cannot communicate consent for the activity."[12]

Research undertaken by the Pennsylvania Coalition Against Rape has resulted in the following statistics:

- Women are 6 times more likely to be victims of elder sexual abuse.
- Only about 30 percent of elderly victims of sexual abuse over the age of 65 years actually report the abuse to the authorities.
- About 83 percent of victims of elder sexual abuse reside in an institutional care center, such as a nursing home.
- About 27 percent of victims of elder sexual abuse occurred in either the elder's own home or in the perpetrators home.

---

10. "Elder Abandonment," https://elder.findlaw.com/elder-abuse/elder-abandonment.html.

11. "Types of Elder Abuse," https://elder.findlaw.com/elder-abuse/types-of-elder-abuse.html.

12. "Sexual Abuse," https://www.nursinghomeabusecenter.com/elder-abuse/types/sexual-abuse/.

Elder Abuse

- About 80 percent of the time, the perpetrator of elder sexual abuse was the caregiver to the elder.
- About 76 percent of elder sexual abuse victims have had their incident witnessed by another.
- About 67 percent of elder sexual abusers were members of the family.[13]

Indicators of sexual abuse against the elderly may include the following:

- A pelvic injury
- Problems walking or sitting
- Developing a sexually transmitted disease or STD
- Torn, bloody or stained underwear
- Bruises of the genitals or inner thigh
- Bleeding from the anus or genitals
- Irritation or pain of the anus or genitals
- Panic attacks
- Signs of Post-traumatic stress disorder (PTSD)
- Symptoms of agitation
- Social or emotional withdrawal from others
- Engaging in inappropriate, unusual or aggressive sexual activities
- Suicide attempts
- Engaging in unusual or inappropriate actions[14]

---

13. "Sexual Abuse," https://www.nursinghomeabusecenter.com/elder-abuse/types/sexual-abuse/.

14. "Sexual Abuse," https://www.nursinghomeabusecenter.com/elder-abuse/types/sexual-abuse/.

Caregiving May Be the Most Difficult Thing You Ever Do

Caregivers may simply break, run out of steam, and can't do it anymore. Emotional abuse, neglect, and abandonment may be the result of a caregiver so tired and so depressed that he or she no longer has the inner resources to provide anything better. It is no sin to admit caregiving cannot be done anymore!

Back in the 1980s, the term "caregiver dementia" was coined to describe the disorientation, forgetfulness, and depression often experienced by those trying to care for someone with dementia. And it is an apt description! Long-term stress is debilitating. In the best of all possible situations, caregiving is a team effort, with different people shouldering varying loads of responsibility in conjunction with organizations and agencies supplementing their efforts.

Conclusion

It takes a village to care for a person with dementia. Congregations can be watchful and helpful in so many different ways simply by paying attention. And by not being naive. Elder abuse is a horrific problem. Caregiver burnout is real. No one should have to walk this journey alone.

12

Saying Goodbye

> At my age, I'm often asked if I'm frightened of death and my reply is always, I can't remember being frightened of birth.
>
> —PETER USTINOV

DEMENTIA IN MOST OF its forms is a terminal illness. It is an unmistakably clear indicator of our mortality. William Saroyan once said that he hoped God would make an exception in his case. I think we all harbor such hope, but the certainty of death presaged by dementia reveals most of our thoughts about death to be thinly disguised denial.

On Death and Dying

Elisabeth Kübler-Ross, a Swiss-born psychiatrist, was the author of the groundbreaking book *On Death and Dying* (1969), in which she proposed five stages of grief: denial, anger, bargaining, depression, and acceptance. In general, individuals experience most of these stages, though not in a clearly defined sequence, after being faced with the reality of their impending death. The five stages apply to the survivors of a loved one's death, as well. And they apply to the caregivers of those who have been told they have dementia.

A television news segment on *60 Minutes* (August 12, 2018) about Alzheimer's disease included interviews with a man whose wife had been diagnosed with Alzheimer's. These interviews took place over the course of ten years. Early on, the husband strongly avows that he will never put his wife in a nursing home. After more than a decade of dealing with her decline, he finally decides to do so. It takes time to get from denial to acceptance.[1]

Death from something like Alzheimer's disease is a slow process. As one of our older men recently told me, "I've been told I have dementia, but chances are that I'll die of something else before it gets too bad." His attitude is one I'd like to emphasize. As much as this book has been about a terrible disease process, it is also about living with that disease process. Much love, much joy, and many good memories can be had between a loved one's diagnosis and his or her death.

Dementia Grief

Dr. Kesstan Blandin has written:

> Grief is a universal experience and response to significant loss. Psychologically, grief is complex, involving several distinct emotions: denial, anger, sadness and heartbreak, guilt, despair or loss of hope, acceptance, love, and joy. These last emotions may surprise you, but people commonly feel love for the person they have lost and great joy at having had that love during grieving. Dementia is a unique disease process that creates an unusual situation: the person with dementia gradually recedes from their loved ones while still alive.[2]

As she goes on to point out, dementia patients die two deaths—the first being the slow psychological elimination of the

---

1. "Following a Couple from Diagnosis."
2. Blandin, "Dementia Grief."

person they had been, and the second being their actual physical death. This means loved ones experience these two deaths as well.

Congregational support can be invaluable for loved ones dealing with this—if we don't forget! Churches are uniquely positioned to help a family in times of acute need. But long-term ministry is more difficult. It wears on friends and neighbors just as it does caregivers.

Disenfranchised Grief

Disenfranchised Grief is a term I had not heard before I delved into the world of dementia. It refers to grief that is not publicly acknowledged and sanctioned. To go back to Blandin's article:

> This can occur in a variety of situations in which there is significant loss of some sort but not the opportunity to talk about it openly because of stigma or lack of understanding and sympathy from others. Disenfranchised grief can occur in the parents of adult children with mental illness, criminality, alcoholism, or other substance abuse. Parents commonly talk about experiencing disenfranchised grief following a miscarriage, or a terminated pregnancy.[3]

Because the loved one is still alive, it is hard to talk about those aspects of the person that are now gone. Church members can be encouraged not to "too quickly" tell caregivers how lucky they are to still have the loved one with them. It is important to remember that the loved one "still there" is not the same person he or she once was.

Ambiguous Loss

A term related to disenfranchised grief is "ambiguous loss," which refers to a loss that lacks clarity and does not have a normal sense of closure.

---

3. Blandin, "Dementia Grief."

There are two types of ambiguous loss. In the first, the individual is physically absent but remains psychologically present. This has been described as "Leaving without saying goodbye." Examples include prisoners of war or those missing in action, victims of disasters such as September 11 whose family were unable to recover a body to bury, or even the absence of a parent due to divorce. In the second type of ambiguous loss, the individual remains physically present, but is psychologically absent—this is described as, "The goodbye without leaving" . . . It is very difficult to grieve someone who may no longer be psychologically present as a spouse, a parent, a companion or other intimate, but who remains very much a physical presence with ever-increasing needs for care that must be met. The very ambiguity of the relationship makes it challenging for the family member to acknowledge the loss, to grieve, and move forward. Since the person with the disease usually changes so gradually, it is not possible for the family member to determine a specific point at which the loved one is really no longer who he once was.[4]

The Importance of Remembering

As the wife of one of my dearest friends was dying, he turned to me and said something like, "Looking at her now it is hard to believe that she once traveled the world. She rode an elephant in India and climbed to the top of one of the pyramids in Egypt. She went everywhere and did everything." He spent the next few hours telling me all about her (even though I had known her for as long as I had known him). He was remembering. Illness had changed her. The personality of the woman he had fallen in love with had disintegrated, but by recalling their life together, she was somehow restored, if only for a brief while.

Frederick Buechner wrote a lovely piece entitled "Remember."

---

4. Blandin, "Dementia Grief."

> When you remember me, it means that you have carried something of who I am with you, that I have left some mark of who I am on who you are. It means that you can summon me back to your mind even though countless years and miles may stand between us. It means that if we meet again, you will know me. It means that even after I die, you can still see my face and hear my voice and speak to me in your heart. For as long as you remember me, I am not entirely lost.[5]

There is a metaphor found in the Bible that is important here: to be "cut off from the land of the living." Sometimes this simply means to die, or even to be exiled. But in Jeremiah 11:19 it refers to a person "whose name will be remembered no more." The irony of persons with dementia is that they may get to the place where they do not know who they are, but we who know them and love them do. While they are still alive we keep their story going by reminding them and others and ourselves about it. And we keep them in the land of the living by remembering them after death. Just because a person's life ends with dementia does not mean that that person's life did not—does not—matter.

About Death

There were at least three convictions on life after death in the first century. First, among Jews, it was thought that there would be a general resurrection of the body at the end of time. Our resurrected bodies would be identical with our earthly bodies. Second, Greeks and Romans often thought of life after death as taking "disembodied" form. If there was such a thing it was a ghostly, ethereal existence. Third, some people suspected that death simply meant extinction. Life as we know it was all there was.

New Testament writers described Christ's resurrection as something similar to Jewish and Greek ideas, but as something that was also different. Emphasis was placed on the physical, worldly reality of the risen Jesus. He was the same Jesus they had

---

5. Buechner, *Whistling in the Dark*, 110.

known before his death. He was recognizable. He talked, walked, ate, and was touched. He was no ghost or phantom. But he was also different. He didn't seem bound by the same physical limitations that those of us experience. In 1 Corinthians 15 Paul wrestled with these contradictory traits: "The body that is sown is perishable, it is raised imperishable; it is sown in dishonor, it is raised in glory; it is sown in weakness, it is raised in power; it is sown a natural body, it is raised a spiritual body."

The Resurrection of Jesus

As uncertain as this attempt to explain the unexplainable is, what is clear is that no New Testament author ever pretended that death isn't so bad after all. Dead is dead. It is the absence of life. God alone is immortal. If there is life beyond death for us, it is not because we possess in ourselves some immortal quality death cannot destroy, but because God gives us this life. It is not because we are strong enough to conquer death, but because God is, and because God in Christ Jesus has triumphed over death for us. Life after death is a gift from God. It is a gift of God based solely on God's grace!

Thus, the resurrection of Jesus is a clue for our own future: because he rose from the dead, we too will also rise. Paul wrote in 1 Thessalonians that he did not want those to whom he was writing to "grieve like those who have no hope." He affirmed that death is not the final word on our existence. Even as Christ was raised from the dead by the power of God, we too will somehow, someway participate in a resurrection like his.

However the Christian hope for life after death is expressed, there is more to it than the hope for a general resurrection at the end of time; there is more to it than an ethereal, ghostly existence; and it is certainly not extinction.

Because we have this hope for a future in Christ Jesus, our remembering of loved ones, even those loved ones who died with dementia, is qualitatively different from that of those who remember without this hope.

Saying Goodbye

Death Is Not the Final Word

There are violent deaths, there are accidental deaths, and sometimes bad things happen for no reason other than the fact that we are human beings. Pain, heartache, grief, loss, disease, and death are inevitable parts of the human experience. Arteries clog, blood clots form, wounds do not heal, procedures designed to cure go awry, and strokes and disease cause dementia. Certain struggles and uncertain results are an innate part of life. There are no exceptions to this rule. We are human and we are fragile. But the vagaries of this life are not the final word on who we are. Neither death nor life, nor anything else in all creation, can separate us from the love of God in Jesus Christ, our Lord, who is the resurrection and the life.

The way to say goodbye to those we've loved, the way to honor their lives and their faith, is to affirm our faith that death is not the final word of our existence. Through our belief in the resurrection we affirm that even as Christ was raised from the dead by the power of God, we too will somehow, someway participate in a resurrection like his. Christ was the first fruit, we the latter fruit. We really do believe that our loved ones are alive in the presence of God, and that we too will someday join them. Those with dementia will have a future redeemed self.

Conclusion

Years ago, when I was a graduate student, I remember the young son of one of my fellow students, asking his father, "What does love have to do with death?" Easter was upon us and he was working hard to put together the pieces of everything he had been hearing. For a person with dementia, death can be a friend. For a tired caregiver, death can bring relief. Not everything about death is to be fought against. In fact, if as Christians we believe what we confess most Sunday mornings—*I believe in the resurrection of the body and the life everlasting*—then in many ways death can be welcomed.

Do Not Cast Me Away

My friend and mentor, Phil Bembower, once told me that death was just another part of living, one that can't be avoided. He said it was simply a way to a different kind of life. By God's grace, in Jesus Christ, it is simply a way to a different kind of life.

Penultimate Thoughts

> To encounter Christ is to touch reality and experience transcendence. He gives us a sense of self-worth or personal significance, because He assures us of God's love for us. He sets us free from guilt because He died for us and from paralyzing fear because He reigns. He gives meaning to marriage and home, work and leisure, personhood and citizenship.
>
> —JOHN STOTT

A Recap

WORKING WITH A SENIOR pastor recovering from a severe brain injury led me to wonder about the broader arena of dementia and all of its causes. (There are more of them than I ever thought possible.) I still have unanswered questions. Some of them are businesslike: What do HR departments do if it is suspected that an employee—or an owner—or a pastor—has dementia? What do hospitals do if a surgeon is suspected of having dementia? Once upon a time one of our presidents may have held office while in the early stages of Alzheimer's. I'm not sure the twenty-fifth amendment to our Constitution will be much help if it happens again and is more advanced.

Some of my questions are medical: Exactly what causes Alzheimer's disease? Can it be avoided? Can it be reversed? Is there any truth in the myriad of articles floating around the internet touting remedies? Or the benefits of this program or that one? And what about the other illnesses that result in dementia? Are we any closer to curing Lewy body dementia? Or corticobasal degeneration?

Some of my questions are philosophical: What is memory? Not just how it works (which we really still don't know), but what is it? Why is it? What does it mean to our humanity if it is impaired?

I even have legal questions: What determines legal competence? How can we know (for sure) what a person with dementia intends for his or her care, or for the distribution of an estate?

But most of my concerns are pastoral: What is the best course of action a family should take if it thinks it is time to take the car keys away from an aging parent slipping into the early stages of dementia? Or the checkbook? Or even their home?

How does one watch for elder abuse? What are the signs of such? How does one guard the best interests of a person who no longer cares or even knows he or she is being taken advantage of or is being ill-treated? On the other hand, how does one guard against false accusations?

What about options for care? What is the best choice? How does one pay for what is often extraordinarily expensive care? How does one balance what a dementia patient needs with the needs of a caregiver? Or the needs of the rest of the family? How does a congregation provide love and support in meaningful and truly helpful ways?

I have no real answers except to hope that the information provided in this book has de-mystified a few of the problems of dealing with dementia and provided some guidance toward viable options for consideration. I hope you find support for the task ahead of you. And I hope you are a member of a congregation that intentionally engages in helping you help your loved one.

Penultimate Thoughts

Remembrance

Elie Wiesel argued passionately that recollection—remembrance—is a moral enterprise.[1] Remembrance gives "voice" to those who have been silenced. Wiesel's anguish was for those killed in the Holocaust, whose voices were prematurely silenced by evil. I suggest we are just now beginning to comprehend how many voices are being silenced by dementia. Surely it is a moral enterprise to remember them! We must remember that those who are demented, even those who are extremely so, are persons. Not were persons, but are. To be human is to forget as well as to remember.

Memory and Personhood

I was surfing the internet one afternoon when I ran across a blog post entitled "Without Memory, Who Are We?" It began this way:

> Remembering is actually central to all of life, although something we often take for granted. It is when we see someone robbed of their memory that we get insight into the importance of remembering. If someone we love is involved in an accident and receives a head injury, one of the things that most concerns us is, "Will they be able to remember anything?" Without memory, who are we?[2]

This is a question I asked in chapter 4. What does it mean to be human? Augustine argued that it was a hidden memory of God within each of us that enables us to recognize encounters with God in the first place. Does it follow that those without memory, or with severely impaired memory, have no basis with which to experience God?

Miroslav Volf, on the other hand, desperately wants to "remember correctly" (without pain and anger) in order to find true reconciliation with those who hurt him in the past. For him, remembering what happened was a hindrance to his own salvation.

---

1. Wiesel wrote about this in many places, one of which is *Night*, viii.
2. Hosier, "Without Memory, Who Are We?"

But Volf did not despair over his explorations into memory. What he did was find a way for us to understand the personhood even of those so demented as to be unable to remember their own names.

Ben Myers, in the book review on Volf's *The End of Memory* that I cited in chapter 4, sums up:

> While it is often said that we would lose our identities if we ceased to remember, Volf draws on Luther's anthropology to present an alternative construal of personal identity. We receive our identity from "outside ourselves;" we are located *in God*, and our identity is found in him.[3]

You see, we don't have to remember who we are in order to be human beings. We don't have to have a fully functioning set of faculties. Dementia does not take away our personhood because our identity, our personhood, is located in Jesus Christ. We are who we are *in him*.

In worship services we sometimes sing *Jesus, remember me, when you come into your kingdom*. This is ultimately where we hang our hat: he remembers us. No matter what, he remembers us. We are who we are in him.

Memory Works Both Ways

My wife told me one morning that she had had a bad dream. She saw herself in a room with the children of a dear friend who had recently died. She was by herself in a corner while the children were looking at photo albums filled with pictures of their deceased mother. She said she cried as she watched them, realizing how she had been alone in another city grieving their mother while they, at least, had each other. Then she said her friend "came to her" and comforted her.

When she told me this I thought of how therapeutic memories can be. I often tell families at funerals to tell each other all the stories they can think of about their loved ones. It is my prayer that

---

3. Myers, "Miroslav Volf."

such stories will bring them some measure of relief from their pain and might even cause a smile to lessen their burden.

With dementia patients, another dimension is also at work. As they lose their memories, we become the ones who remember. We tell them who they are, where they are, how they've lived, and what they did. Finally, when they are gone, after we have worked through our grief, it is our memories of them that provide us with comfort. It is as though—through our memories of them—they are able to "come to us" and give back to us what they are able to give, which is exactly the thing they have lost. No one is cut off from the land of the living while we remember them.

Sing from Memory (Again)

On August 21, 2018, twenty-five or so volunteers from Northside Presbyterian Church in Chattanooga, Tennessee, gathered in what is known as "the community room" for a dress rehearsal for Sing from Memory.

Four "teams" went through the motions of welcoming those with dementia and their caregivers to our church. Temporary signs went up, marking the way. Ushers stood outside to guide persons into the building. Greeters were ready with magic markers and name tags. Simple snacks and drinks were on a table. And song leaders had a program of downloaded videos of "old favorites" (with lyrics) to supplement the hymns our pianist was prepared to play.

For nearly two hours we sang and laughed together as we fumbled our way through video after video and hymn after hymn. My wife and I had been charged with coming up with a sort of an entertaining interlude halfway through the music. We did the hokey-pokey for movement, popped bubble wrapping for arthritic fingers, and asked "finish this line" questions.

On September 4, we went live! It was glorious. We only had four or five persons with dementia, along with four or five caregivers, but with so many of our own members present, no one stood out and, honestly, no one could tell who was who! One of the first lessons we learned was not to underestimate our guests. When we got to the "finish this line" segment of the program, one man, named John, answered them all. He might not be able to tell you what he had to eat for breakfast, but he knew the ending of every saying we could throw out there.

Since then we have had a floating number of attendees, with some becoming regulars and others dropping in and out. But all the them have heard the same thing from us: they matter. Those with dementia and those caring for them all matter.

The Hard Stuff

The two most difficult sections of this book were chapters 9 (on paying for medical care) and 11 (on elder abuse). While researching how people afford to care for loved ones with dementia, I was continually drawn back into memories I have of families I've worked with. In most cases, it never dawned on me how they paid for it. I was paying attention to how they were doing emotionally. I now see that I overlooked what must have been a tremendous source of anxiety for them. I never asked how they were paying for their loved one's care, but I should have somehow expressed concern over it. I could have given them a chance to vent their frustration (if it was difficult) or express their satisfaction (if they had planned well).

I am better equipped now to guide a family to resources that might be helpful than I have ever been before, and I hope you or your congregation is, too. At the end of this chapter I have included a short list of agencies, websites, and books that I have turned to for your consideration.

The other difficult topic was elder abuse. It is never right. No matter how a caregiver or someone else has been provoked, no matter how ugly or mean a patient has been, no matter how impossible the situation might be, it is never right. But I sure understand, better than ever, how a caregiver could end up being abusive. There but for the grace of God!

At one of our Sing from Memory sessions a man with dementia suddenly stood up and began to move toward the door. His wife, who had been singing along enjoying herself, grudgingly got to her feet and said to me, "When he's ready to go, we go. He won't stay anywhere very long." As she caught up to him in the hallway I wondered what her life was really like. It can't be easy.

No Cure for the Curse (Not Yet, Anyway)

I recently scanned the internet for articles on detecting and/or curing dementias. I found: "A Brian Implant Improved Memory, Scientists Report"; "Calcium Imbalance within Brain Cells May Trigger Alzheimer's Disease"; "Curry May Boost the Brain's Neural Stem Cells"; "Alzheimer's May Be Treated with Diabetes Drugs"; "Eye Scan May Detect Alzheimer's Disease in Seconds"; and "Herpes May Account for 50 Percent of All Alzheimer's Cases."[4] We are terrified of dementia. We are desperate for a cure. But there is none. And as far as I have been able to discern, no cure is realistically on the horizon.

Still, there are things we can do. We can learn a language, keep reasonably fit, stay in contact with our friends (and make new ones), and play an instrument. These are the only things that show even the slightest positive effect in warding off or slowing down dementia.

Also, we can live our lives in such a way that we will be remembered. We can live until we can't live anymore. We can live with such vitality and such kindness and such love that should we begin to lose our minds, our caregivers will take great pleasure in telling us about ourselves!

We must never forget that our humanity is not found in our heads but in our hearts. Our identity is found in Christ Jesus. It is external to us, gifted upon us. We are God's children. We are who we are in him. Always and forever.

---

4. Corey, "Brain Implant"; Lees, "Curry"; Sandoiu, "Alzheimer's," "Calcium," "Eye Scan"; Railton, "Herpes."

Suggested Resources

Agencies

American Association of Retired People (AARP)
Administration on Aging
Alzheimer's Association
Councils on Aging
Centers for Disease Control
Center for Medicare Advocacy
Centers for Medicare and Medical Services
Dementia Society of America
National Institute on Aging

Books

The 36 Hour Day by Nancy L. Mace and Peter V. Rabins
Aging Together by John and Susan McFadden
Ambiguous Loss by Pauline Boss
Being Mortal by Atul Gwandi
The Good Funeral by Tomas G. Long and Thomas Lynch
Into the Storm: Journeys with Alzheimer's by Collin Tong
Learning to Speak Alzheimer's by Joanne Koenig Coste
Loving Someone Who Has Dementia by Pauline Boss
When Bad Things Happen to Good People by Harold S. Kushner
While I Still Can by Rick Phelps and Gary Joseph Leblanc

Suggested Resources

Websites

agingcare.com
alzheimersreadingroom.com
caring.com
dementia.org
dementiacarestrategies.com
elder.findlaw.com
goldencarers.com
mayoclinic.org
senioradvisor.com

Bibliography

Ansberry, Clare. "The Call to Care for Parents Comes Sooner Now." *Wall Street Journal*, Aug. 6, 2018.

Augustine. *Confessions*. Translated by Henry Chadwick. Oxford: Oxford University Press, 1991.

Barth, Karl. *The Humanity of God*. London: Collins, 1961.

Blandin, Kesstan. "Dementia Grief—Part 1: The Unique Characteristics." https://www.dementia.org/dementia-grief-characteristics.

Buechner, Frederick. *Whistling in the Dark*. San Francisco: HarperCollins, 1993.

Bursack, Carol Bradley. "Unearned Guilt Intrinsic to Most Caregiving." Healthcentral, Nov 12, 2013.

Butts, Calvin. "In the Image of God." Sermon at the conference "America's Music with Wynton Marsalis and Jazz at Lincoln Center," Aug 26, 2016.

Chappell, Bill. "Doctors, Nurses among 243 Charged in Million-Dollar Medicare Schemes." NPR, Jun 19, 2015.

Corey, Benedict. "A Brain Implant Improved Memory, Scientists Report." *New York Time*, Feb 6, 2018.

DeMarco, Bob. "What Is the Virtual Dementia Tour Program?" Alzheimer's Reading Room, Jan 31, 2010.

Dementia Care Practice Recommendations for Assisted Living Residences and Nursing Homes. Chicago: Alzheimer's Association, 2005.

Dr. Bob Show HD Archives. "'Frontotemporal Dementia' with Dr. Monica Crane." *YouTube*, Nov 2, 2018. https://www.youtube.com/watch?v=qM8m5opyNgc.

Esposito, Lisa. "What Nursing Home 'Memory Care' Means." *U.S. News*, Jun 1, 2016.

Foer, Joshua. *Moonwalking with Einstein*. New York: Penguin, 2012.

"Following a Couple from Diagnosis to the Final Stages of Alzheimer's." *60 Minutes*, Aug 12, 2018.

Hamilton, John. "Big Financial Costs Are Part of Alzheimer's Toll on Families." NPR's *Morning Edition*, Mar 30, 2016.

Heimlich, Russell. "Baby Boomers Retire." Pew Research Center, Dec 29, 2010.

Hosier, Matthew. "Without Memory, Who Are We?" *Think* (blog), Apr 22, 2011.

Bibliography

Howley, Elaine K. "Homecare for a Loved One with Alzheimer's or Dementia." *U.S. News*, Jun 19, 2019.

Jenkins, Sally. "Pat Summit, Tennessee Women's Basketball Coach, Diagnosed with Alzheimer's Disease." *Washington Post*, Aug 23, 2011.

Juliano, Stephen. "Coping with Guilt after Moving Your Senior Loved One" Presbyterian Senior Living, Jan 4, 2018.

Larsen, Dana. "The De Hogeweyk Dementia Care Revolution." A Place for Mom, Jun 14, 2013.

Lees, Kathleen. "Curry May Boost the Brain's Neural Stem Cells." ScienceWorldReport, Sep 26, 2014.

Marcus, Mary Brophy. "Some Caring for Alzheimer's Patients Make 'Startling' Sacrifices." CBS News, Mar 30, 2016.

McFadden, Susan H., and John T. McFadden. *Aging Together: Dementia, Friendship, and Flourishing Communities*. Baltimore: Johns Hopkins University Press, 2011.

McLeod, Saul. "Multi Store Model of Memory." https://www.simplypsychology.org/multi-store.html.

Myers, Ben. "Miroslav Volf: The End of Memory." Faith and Theology, May 12, 2007.

Ostrov, Barbara Feder. "Why Long-Term Care Insurance Is Becoming a Tougher Call." http://money.com/money/4250147/long-term-care-insurance-rising-premiums/.

Presbyterian Senior Living. *Clearing up Differences between Non-Profit and For-Profit Senior Living Organizations*. Ebook. Dillsboro, PA. https://www.presbyterianseniorliving.org/differences-between-non-profit-for-profit-senior-living-organizations.

Railton, David. "Herpes May Account for 50 Percent of All Alzheimer's Cases." *Medical News Today*, Oct 19, 2018.

Rashi. *Commentary on Genesis*. https://www.sefaria.org/Rashi_on_Genesis?lang=bi.

Rosengren, John. "7 Ways to Prevent Financial Elder Abuse." AARP Bulletin, Aug 29, 2018.

Sandoiu, Ana. "Alzheimer's May Be Treated with Diabetes Drugs." *Medical News Today*, Nov 5, 2018.

———. "Calcium Imbalance within Brain Cells May Trigger Alzheimer's Disease." *Medical News Today*, Feb 15, 2017.

———. "Eye Scan May Detect Alzheimer's Disease in Seconds." *Medical News Today*, Oct 30, 2018.

"The Scots Confession of 1560." In *Book of Confessions*. N.p.: Presbyterian Church (USA), 1999.

Welsh, Daniel. "Robin Williams' Widow, Susan, Gives First Interview Since Actor's Death, Insists 'Depression Did Not Kill Him.'" *Huffington Post*, Mar 11, 2015.

Whitbourne, Susan Krauss. "The Definitive Guide to Guilt." *Psychology Today*, Aug 11, 2012.

Bibliography

Whitworth, Hellen Buell, and James Whitworth. *A Caregiver's Guide to Lewy Body Dementia*. New York: Demos Health, 2011.

Wiesel, Elie. *Night*. New York: Hill and Wang, 2006.

Yosuico, Isabella. "Tips for Long Distance Caregivers." https://www.care.com/c/stories/5594/tips-for-long-distance-caregivers/.

Zamora, Amanda. "Life and Death in Assisted Living: Seven Questions to Ask When Searching for Assisted Living." ProPublica, Jul 31, 2013.

www.ingramcontent.com/pod-product-compliance
Lightning Source LLC
Chambersburg PA
CBHW070500090426
42735CB00012B/2630